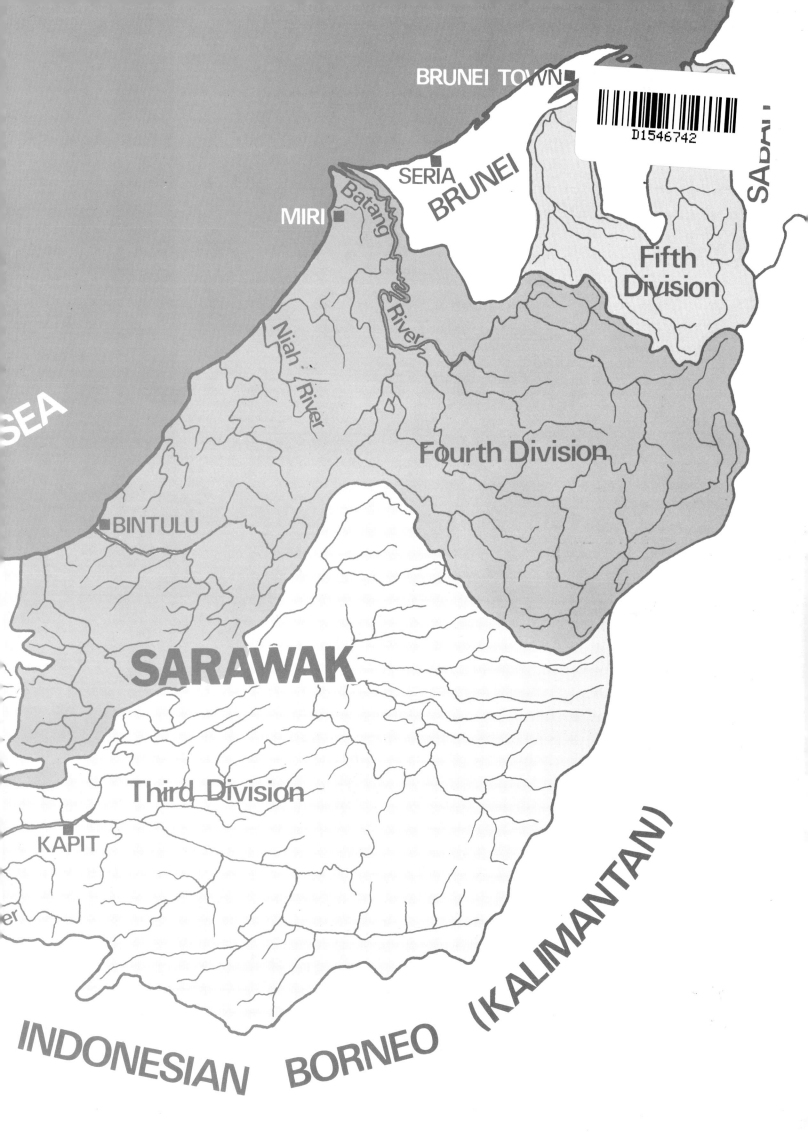

Vanishing World

Vanishing World

THE IBANS OF BORNEO

Leigh Wright
Hedda Morrison
K.F. Wong

WEATHERHILL/SERASIA
NEW YORK ■ TOKYO ■ HONG KONG

Credits: *Black-and white-photographs by Hedda Morrison.
Color photographs by K. F. Wong, except those on pages
16, 17, 65, 88, and 89, which are by Nigel Cameron. Photographs on pages 21, 31, 33, 68, 81, and 101 are reproduced
by permission of the Director, Borneo Literature Bureau.*

First Edition, 1972

Jointly published by John Weatherhill, Inc., 149 Madison
Avenue, New York, New York 10016, with editorial offices
at 7-6-13 Roppongi, Minato-ku, Tokyo 106; and Serasia Ltd.,
Asian House, 1 Hennessy Road, Wanchai, Hong Kong.
Copyright © 1971 by Serasia Ltd.; all rights reserved. Printed
in Japan.

LCC Card No. 75-162686 ISBN 0-8348-1851-5

CONTENTS

THE SETTING

Three or four decades ago, every schoolboy in Britain knew about the White Rajah who owned a land of headhunters in Borneo, ruled the natives with kindliness, and lived in strange splendor in that somewhat grisly but fascinating jungle paradise. When these former British school-boys and schoolgirls grew up, they probably recalled only that, and little more about Borneo.

After World War II was over and the newspapers of Britain carried front page stories of how the British government was about to take over the White Rajah's land and make it into a crown colony, and how the rajah was engaged in a dispute with the Government, probably most people were emotionally on the side of the rajah. Memories, dormant since childhood, revived, and it seemed a shame that Rajah Brooke (even though he had indicated his desire to turn the place over to the authorities in Whitehall) should not get fair compensation at least for a property his family had so long ruled, to the glory of Britain and the edification of romantic British Empire enthusiasts.

Thus, in the middle of the twentieth century, Sarawak and its ideal-ized tribes again disturbed the public conscience, and all those hoary old notions from centuries before about 'noble savages' came up for discussion once more.

Until the middle of the nineteenth century, Borneo was a name hardly known to the West. Despite the fact that Borneo is the world's third—some say fourth—largest island, its peoples, its gamut of flora and fauna, and the life of its jungles lay, and even now to some extent still lie, off the beaten track.

The Chinese had discovered coastal Borneo many centuries ago, and had set up one or two trading stations where small expatriate com-munities lived. Death, as in many another community where little written or monumental evidence has come down to us, is more revealing than life; and in Sarawak on the northern coast of Borneo, one or two Chinese cemeteries have been excavated in recent years and tell their tale through the porcelain and gold ornaments buried with the de-ceased members of those tiny communities. The Chinese came in search of birds' nests, spices, and possibly gold. To this day, one of the more expensive exports of Sarawak is the nest of the swiftlet, so prized by Chinese everywhere as the principal ingredient of a special soup. One other perhaps even more exotic product of Borneo tempted the Chinese to the far shores of the island—the bossed beak and frontal portion of the head of the *kenyalang* bird, commonly called the hornbill. This 'ivory' was exported to China and carved into all manner of delicate and intricate patterns and sculptural shapes. From these early times—from the glorious T'ang dynasty of the seventh to ninth century onward—there is little but scanty Chinese records in which the island is named, and the pathetic little cemeteries of those overseas Chinese.

It was not until A. R. Wallace, a naturalist of the mid-nineteenth century whose theory of evolution was partly worked out while he lived in Borneo, acquired a certain fame that the island attracted some public notice. At that time, too, the novelist Joseph Conrad was writing about Borneo in his tales of the East, and probably it was these romantic adventure stories that did as much as or more than any other event to bring Borneo into the uncertain focus of the Western public eye. Even

The morning mist lingers over the jungle trees. Dense rainforest covers most of Sarawak

The commonest form of bridge over a stream is a fallen tree, or one that has been deftly felled for the purpose

in the studious days of the nineteenth century, novelists were more widely read than naturalists. Perhaps not until the heyday of Somerset Maugham, with his twisting and deceptive plots about life in the East viewed from the white man's standpoint as the heroic empire builder with built-in problems in his sex life, did something of the jungled reality of far Borneo and its ways strike the West with any force. And even then Borneo was only a backdrop to the vastly important adventures, loves, peccadillos, hates, and hopes of the ruling English.

Most of what has been written on Borneo for the general public tends to be highly romantic, and there is certainly an excuse for that attitude in dealing with such a place. The tales of headhunting warriors, dire acts of piracy around the coasts, and pictures of comely brown-skinned girls happy the livelong day in a cheerful pagan life abound

in the literature. These tales are not without an element of truth—a greater or lesser element depending on what aspect they deal with. But the total picture projected by this material has in fact only a rather slight bearing on the reality of the life and ways of the tribal peoples who inhabit the riverbanks of Borneo's great jungles. The reality is certainly more complicated—as elsewhere in the world—and, for those fortunate travelers who have spent some time on the island and got to know a little of its peoples, infinitely more interesting.

Only since the end of World War II have scholars and scientists and travelers with less romantic and less government-servant minds penetrated far into the world of the Dayaks, as the tribal peoples of the interior are generally called, in a methodical attempt to learn more than is contained in official reports or in tales of adventure. Only recently has

Ibans on the summit of Mount Sepali, the watershed between the Ngemah and Katibas rivers

it been possible to draw something like a rounded picture of life and its hopes and prospects, its changes and its tenacious past—of Dayak life as it is lived by the attractive and in many ways well-integrated people whom history has placed in Borneo.

Despite its position, sitting squarely athwart the equator between latitude 4° south and latitude 7° north, Borneo hardly presents the typical picture of coral strand and palm tree paradise peopled by smiling, sensuous, lackadaisical natives that most of us tend to have of tropical islands. There are, indeed, sandy beaches and coral, and millions of palm trees, but Borneo people, though sensuous enough, as people are in most places, and comelier and nakeder than in some, are not notably idle. Like most of us, they might well prefer to be. But most of us find we can't actually live in idleness.

About the size of Norway and Sweden put together, most of Borneo's 288,000 square miles are covered with a dense coating of rain forest—a tangled growth and intergrowth of trees, vines, creepers, and shrubs, much of it not virgin forest but secondary jungle. From the air, this vast woolly green rug of land heaves up in ridges and sinks to valleys that contain swift little dashing streams. The ridges and folds of the land rise to mountain ranges from 3,000 to 6,000 feet high and rear up majestically, losing their verdure, to over 13,000 feet at Mt. Kinabalu in Sabah in the north. The mountains are the watersheds of the large network of rivers that flow east and south to join the Celebes and Java seas, and westward to the South China Sea. The land falls and flattens in fairly gentle gradients toward the northern coasts, crossed by long ocherous rivers meandering like the lines between the pieces of a jigsaw

Hauling a perahu *upstream at the rapids. The outboard motor is shipped to prevent damage*

The lower reaches of the rivers are tortuous and sluggish, overhung by huge jungle trees

The women are generally first to emerge from the longhouse in the early morning, going down to the river to wash

The Entabai River runs through a tunnel of foliage. The tree on the left is overgrown with orchids

puzzle. And at the sea the shoreline is often swamp where mangrove and sago palms are almost the only significant vegetation that thrives. There are, to be sure, some magnificent sandy beaches miles and miles long, but not very many.

The mountains are the watershed, but their other function has been to divide the island geographically, and also by inhabited regions, into two—the larger part lying south and east of them and the smaller (about one-quarter of the island) to the northwest. In recent times the same ranges of mountains have become a political divide between the larger part that was claimed by the Dutch in the 17th century and is now part of Indonesia, and the smaller part that, in one of history's more romantic tales, fell into the hands of the White Rajah Brooke, and eventually British colonialism, in the nineteenth century. Recently this part,

consisting of Sarawak and Sabah, joined Malaya to form the new state of Malaysia.

The winding rivers of Borneo are and always have been all-important to the people who live there. Riverine living has been the necessity that has shaped life. In a land so impenetrably covered by jungle, and so hilly, crosscountry communication was, and in most places still is, slow and arduous. It is often quicker to descend many miles by river, make a short flat-country journey, and ascend equally far along another river, than to attempt to go direct along the straightest line between your starting point and destination. There are a few roads nowadays, and more are being built. From an airplane they look like little pinkish arteries, small and feeble in comparison with the majestic meanders of the broad rivers.

The rapids are often small waterfalls, and boats have to be carried. Kayan hats are favored by the boatmen

For this reason among others, the villages of the Dayaks have always been on riverbanks or within walking distance of rivers, or at river mouths and coastal creeks. Rivers are the highways, their fish a source of food, their waters the reservoirs and bathing places. Thus the Borneo peoples, like their cousins in the Malay peninsula, evolved as a riverine society.

There is hardly a pleasanter experience in life, for those so inclined, than to take a small ramshackle Chinese motor vessel and chug along the coast of Sarawak to the mouth of one of the smaller rivers. Disembarking there, you transfer to a smaller boat for the journey upstream. In former days—in fact until the years just after World War II—most of the river boats were paddled, but now only the smallest *perahu*s, as the slips of canoes are called, are without the outboard engines that—

alas!—destroy much of the millennial calm that pervades the scene.

Only a decade ago, as you paddled upriver, it was quite usual to come upon a Chinese junk. A great bulgy black-painted hulk suddenly loomed round one of the bends, taking up most of the river's width. At dusk when the light is low and eerie, the sky a mere pale strip stretched between the tops of the tall tree precipices that enclose the river, the huge eyes painted in white, one on either side of the junk's bows, gave it the appearance of some elephantine creature from the dawn of the world's time—an experience quite in keeping with the moment and with the surroundings. For time, even nowadays on the Borneo rivers, seems to have stopped a long way back, at a period when the luxuriance of nature as it straddled the surface of the globe was still untamed and undisturbed by man the toolmaker. It was, and you can see how it still

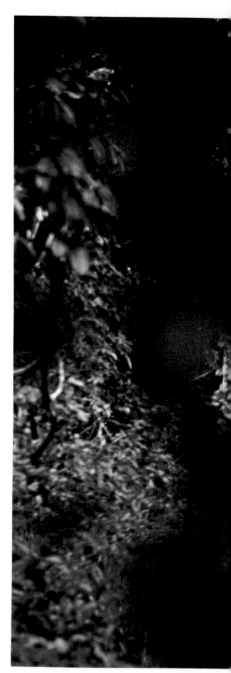

A little girl in a sling on her mother's back

This man's pierced earlobes have stretched with the weight of his earrings

A young Iban beauty

Women paddling a small perahu *used for very short trips*

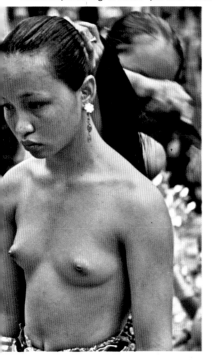

Father and child. The pierced earlobes and tattoos are typical

Cooking a meal near Kapit on the upper Rajang River

is in Borneo, a time of rampant trees, of the deadly struggle for survival between tree and tree, plant and plant, and animal and animal.

Flaunting scarlet butterflies whose wing-span is over nine inches, flag their way along the riverbanks, tasting here and there the succulence of huge hibiscus and the tiny flowers that are much more common in jungle surroundings. A sudden infuriated scramble and a flutter of leaves and twigs pinpoint a colony of monkeys ripping their way through paths in the treetops, screeching with rage or delight, you hardly know which. And the chorus of the sunset cicadas rings like some carillon of tiny but insistent bells.

In daytime the scene is more animated, the sun striking down, often between piles of brilliant white cloud. The river is generally alive with boats of all kinds: every size of narrow *perahu*, paddled or driven by outboard motor, and fast government launches zooming upriver and trailing strong washes that set the smaller boats rocking and pitching. Now and then a tugboat comes slowly downstream, trailing behind it a long series of rafts made of great treetrunks loosely tied together. Timber extraction these days is a major source of income in Borneo and large areas have been set aside for this apparently destructive business. There are, too, a few shapeless ferry boats with tin canopies, which are used by local people to make their way to some village on the river too far away for their own craft, where Chinese shops sell all manner of things from Petromax lamps to sewing cotton, from cigarettes to vegetables and cheap flashy watches.

Here and there, especially in the early morning, the women of some village concealed by the trees are washing themselves and their clothes,

Fishing with a conical casting net called a jala

and the children are splashing and laughing. The young women are modest and keep their sarongs tied under the armpits as they bathe, but the old ones sit contentedly in the shallows, naked from the waist up, leathery and withered, their hair screwed up in graying knots. The old times when all the girls were bare breasted have gone, and the favored dress is now the traditional sarong tied around the waist, and an inappropriate Western-style brassiere. The menfolk are less modest and plunge in naked, glistening in the sun. The Iban and other Dayak tribal groups are well-made people, formed from childhood by walking and climbing and swimming in the rivers.

There is little danger of crocodiles in the lower reaches of Borneo's rivers, for these tend to inhabit the headwaters. The only hazard is an occasional bore, a wall of water driven upriver from the wide estuary when the spring tides there prevent the inflow of seawater from running back to the ocean. Often several feet high, the bore sweeps up the river with a loud roaring sound, carrying before it the villagers' boats and often drowning unwary bathers as it passes. Somerset Maugham saw one and with his usual dramatic ingenuity used it in the central episode of his story "The Yellow Streak."

The rivers are as vital to the life of the Borneo people as they are infinite in the variety of sights they afford. Some of the larger ones are navigable for long distances from the mouth, provided always that the vessels are of shallow enough draught to cross the sandbar there at high tide. The Rajang, largest river of Sarawak, is navigable for 150 miles, up to Kapit some 70 miles past Sibu, the country's second biggest city.

Rock formations inside the Niah Caves. Apertures in the ceiling let in shafts of sunlight

Tiang *(poles) in the Niah Caves, climbed in order to reach the swiftlet nests used in birds' nest soup*

A village shop at Meluan in the Kanowit district. Ibans bring their home-grown rubber and exchange it for the goods they want

Crossing the bar is in itself often a hazardous and an exciting experience. Lurching along the coast, the boat slows down as the ridge of sea indicating the line of the sandbar comes into view. The pilot cranes his head forward and swings the wheel as his assistant shades his eyes to find what seems to be the most propitious place for the crossing. Since the sandbar alters from season to season, and even from tide to tide, each crossing is a new navigational problem. Then, at a cry from the lookout, the helmsman whirls the old wooden steering wheel and rings down to the engineman for full speed. The old tub heads for the selected place, passengers and crew alike tense for the moment of crossing as the ridge in the sea approaches. It is a lucky day when the boat sweeps over with only a heave on the wave. If not, a series of sickening bumps that make everything shudder reverberate

through the superstructure. Everyone prays that the propeller does not get damaged—and the boat wallows over into the lagoonlike calm inshore. On the unluckiest days the boat is quite likely to end up battered to pieces amid its own oil slick.

A trip upriver reveals not only the sights and sounds of the jungle and the life of the country, but also a cross section of Borneo people. At the river mouth there is usually a large village or small town—a collection of ramshackle one- or two-story shophouses (as they are called in Southeast Asia) lining the bank, with a footpath of timber or just of muddy earth running in front of it, and a jetty or two with a fringe of boats tied up. Most of the shops consist of open-fronted rooms stuffed with the multifarious goods the local people buy. Some are fruit and vegetable stores, some sell spare parts for outboard motors,

Examining a memory tablet whose series of pictographs represents the sequence of a ritual

others sell dried goods such as the numerous varieties of Chinese mushrooms and root vegetables. Sometimes you will see young girls and old women sitting outside a shop on the sidewalk scraping at strange grayish objects about the size of a child's hand. These are birds' nests gathered by the Iban Dayaks and others from the dark interiors of caves upcountry; and the process of cleaning them, removing feathers and other impurities, is a slow and painstaking job. Later the nests will be exported to Singapore and as far as China itself to satisfy the Chinese craving for the kind of soup of which they are the major ingredient. This activity must be at least a thousand years old.

In these village shops—all of them run by Chinese—most of the Ibans and others have accounts, meticulously kept in Chinese characters by the owner of the store. The Dayaks are frequently in debt to the Chinese—a fact that sometimes makes for local discord. In the shops you will see people of various tribes—Ibans and perhaps even one or two men of other groups, such as the Kelabits, from remote places. It depends on the particular river. There are generally Malays—often darker in skin coloration than the Dayaks and Chinese, the women wearing the short, almost transparent Malay jacket over a sarong. Even Chinese in Borneo have taken to the sarong for everyday wear—something that would surprise their compatriots in the homeland far to the north. And the Chinese character, too, has been modified in many ways by long divorce from its traditional area. Shopping in the villages is a long, conversational process in which to hurry is unthought of and of which a snack in the local restaurant is the natural conclusion.

Here and there on the way up the river are other villages, very similar but generally smaller, often shaded by huge trees so that inside the shops it seems dark. Malays are fewer in the interior, and the predominant tribal group living around that particular river makes up the bulk of the population.

Toward the source, the rapids begin and the river narrows, sometimes completely overhung by trees forming a tall gothic arch under whose canopy the midday sun glows green on the clear water. And finally there is nothing for it but to disembark and walk to your destination, for not even a *perahu* can penetrate farther.

There are no distinct physical demarcation lines dividing the places where the various Borneo peoples live. The people can be divided very roughly into three main groups: the Malays, who are Moslems, and many of whom claim fairly recent descent from immigrants from the Malay peninsula; the Chinese, who are mostly shopkeepers, pepper farmers, and, in the towns, clerks and mechanics; and the Dayaks. Besides these there are several smallish groups of itinerant peoples, including the Bugis and recent immigrants from Java and Sumatra who may indeed have settled in Borneo but who are not generally identified with the three large groups.

Malays make up rather less than a third of the population, and they have tended to stay on the coast or on the lower reaches of large rivers. Some of them are farmers and have been there for a long time, but most are town dwellers. Traditionally they have been the rulers of the rivers, their right to rule deriving from the strategic position of their villages at the river mouths and from equally strategic alliances with Malay settlements on neighboring rivers. In Borneo almost anyone can become a Moslem, and many Dayak tribal peoples have become Malays in this way.

By far the most heterogeneous of the three large groups, and certainly the most fascinating, is the Dayaks. The word 'Dayak' is a generic term used loosely to denote any of the large number of pagan tribal peoples and communities. These differ from each other quite as much as they differ from Malays and Chinese. Europeans and Borneans alike distinguish the energetic and vigorous Sea Dayaks, or Ibans, of Sarawak and western Borneo (what is now Indonesian Kalimantan), from the Land Dayaks who occupy a small southwestern patch of Borneo near the capital, Kuching. The latter are slower and less sophisticated jungle dwellers than the Ibans. The kayans and the Kenyahs of north-eastern Sarawak, in their turn, have more in common with each other than either has with the Land or Sea Dayaks. Then there are the lowland-dwelling Dusuns, the hill-country Muruts in Sabah and Brunei, and the Klemantans of Indonesian Borneo. Smaller groups such as Melanaus are Moslems and Christians. The Bajaus or Sea Gypsies also have their place in the pattern of peoples, as does the tiny group of Punans, little people, nomadic, and true hill-jungle dwellers. There are, too, the Kelabits, mountain people of a more settled type.

In origin, all the Dayaks are of mainland Asian stock and have Mongol characteristics in common with other peoples of Southeast Asia. The differences among them are probably the result of migrations at different periods and by different routes. Next to the Chinese and Malays, the Ibans consider themselves to be the most recent arrivals. The centers and migratory routes of most of those groups are fairly well known once they reached Borneo.

Here on the great tangled island of Borneo all these varied and in many ways astonishing peoples live nowadays in comparative harmony. It has not always been so. To understand something of the character of the Ibans, of their curious but valid way of life, and of how they came to adapt to their environment with all its problems and pleasures, we have to separate the various aspects of topography, history, beliefs, and customs and look at the most important and interesting parts of each.

When the Westerners first came to Borneo they had neither the desire nor the skills to do any such thing. They came as strange and powerful men. The origins of 'native' peoples interested few of them, and then merely in the realm of speculation. Western interest was primarily commercial. So the story of the Dayaks, and of the Ibans in particular, was not unraveled until much nearer our own time. The story of the Ibans is both curious and exciting in its details, woven closely as it is into the fabric of events in Borneo—many of the most evocative events, such as the century of rule by the White Rajahs, are so close to us in time yet so far from the social climate of the mid-twentieth century as to read like a page from Conrad.

There were, however, human habitations and communities in Borneo over forty thousand years ago. Their graves and the sites of their hearths under the overhang of cave mouths, and their boats, which closely resemble those on the rivers today, have been dug up in recent years. Rubbish dumps, those revealing archaeological phenomena, have been scientifically picked over, bringing to light the remarkable fact that at that distant Stone Age time the Borneo peoples of the area were eating the same kinds of fish, bats, shellfish, and animals as they do today (or did only yesterday), and that the large mother-of-pearl fastenings of belts seen at various Dayak ceremonies are identical to those worn by their ancestors forty thousand years ago. In Sarawak the Stone Age, or something not far from it, continued into the nineteenth century. What an extraordinary age it was we can discover from the remains of customs and life-styles that persist in Borneo today.

The world of the Ibans and of their fellow tribesmen of Sarawak and Borneo is a vanishing world. In the space of the next two decades the old life will probably have gone for good—in very much the same way as the pastoral world of England celebrated by the poets of the eighteenth century vanished with the age of discovery and the age of machinery. The Borneo world that has endured in all its strangeness and charm, its illogicality and its curious order, in its glorious island setting will disappear much more rapidly.

HISTORY

When James Brooke first met the Iban pirates whom he was to subdue and rule for so long, he noted both their nobility and their savagery. "They are fairer in complexion, superior in stature, and better made than any Dayaks I have seen; their countenances, too, are peculiar,—features good, lips thin, and the eyes small and keen; their bodies are spare, and they bear the air of wild and independent people. Some of their *prahus* carried fifty men, and they plied the paddles with vigour and regularity. They are the most savage of the tribes . . . and delight in head hunting and pillage, whether by sea or land. They reckon all they fall in with as fair prize, and acknowledge no friends but in their own waters: they are faithful to their agreements, hospitable, and, it is reported, kind to strangers . . . ."

It took several years for Brooke to pacify these "wild and independent people," and it was precisely the highly independent nature of the Ibans which was to prove so troublesome to the Brooke rajahs during the whole of their rule in Sarawak. Even today, after over a century of direct contact with European and Chinese colonizers, the Ibans have retained intact their tribal vigor and their identity. That this is so is due partly to the white rajahs. As the second rajah wrote very early during his long life among these Sea Dayaks, "A native should not be permitted to lose pride in himself or his tribe." This attitude set the tone of the native policy of the white rajahs. The policy of paternal benevolence, while wrapping a protective cloak around the Ibans, at the same time largely stifled progress toward modernization of the life of these Borneo pagans.

Modern scholars hold several theories about the origin of the Dayaks. The common thread connecting these theories is that the Dayaks migrated from outside Borneo and arrived at different periods, which varied greatly from one group to another, resulting in great differences in physical characteristics and living habits. Most authorities agree that among the Dayaks the Ibans were latecomers to Borneo. Wallace considered them closely allied racially to the Malayans, and earlier to the Thais and other 'Mongol Asians.' And George W. Earl, a ship's captain from western Australia who sailed the East Indies waters seeking trade, and who stayed on to become an official in Singapore, thought all the Dayaks resembled the Laotians and the Cochin Chinese in physiognomy and language.

The legends of the Ibans themselves recount that they originated in the Middle East and came to Borneo by way of Sumatra. Indeed the migration of some tribes from Sumatra to western Borneo is a well-established fact, and it is thought that some peoples from Sumatra and Java came directly to Point Datu and the vicinity of the Sarawak river. Melanaus here and farther north along the coast may be related to the Ibans by a common ancestry.

By far the largest number of Dayaks migrated to the vicinity of the Kapuas River in the southwest of present-day Kalimantan. And today Ibans, who form the largest single community in Sarawak, trace the main body of migration from Kapuas, although quite a number identify ancestors among the Sumatran arrivals in Sarawak.

The story of the Ibans in Sarawak begins with their ancestors' first migrations over the low hills from the Kapuas River system in Kalimantan (in what is now Indonesian Borneo). The story of this long movement bulks large in the remembered and honored past among Iban communities today. Many a detail is committed to memory and passed on as *tusut,* or family annals. Some of these *tusut* that have

been collected and written down seem to go back as far as thirty generations. Benedict Sandin, curator of the Sarawak Museum and himself an Iban, has done considerable research into *tusut* and was instrumental in bringing these sources to the notice of historians of early Sarawak. The Kapuas migrations probably represented nothing more than an expansionist tendency caused by the search for fresh agricultural land, a general overspill into the region of a large neighboring river system.

The first of the migrants probably arrived at the Undup, Kumpang, and Batang Ai streams in the early or mid-sixteenth century. These streams are tributaries of the Batang Lupar, a magnificent river which is to this day predominantly an Iban area. Expansion continued as small bands settled into the virgin jungles of what is now the Second Division (province) of Sarawak. Thus the pioneering days of the Sarawak Ibans began, and for perhaps a century and a half migration and settlement continued, spreading deeper into Sarawak. Other rivers in the area—the Skrang, Bangat, Saribas, and Rimbas—were also settled, making the surrounding country for a long time the heartland of the energetic and warlike Iban Dayaks. It was on the lower reaches of the Batang Lupar and the Saribas River that the first white rajah, James Brooke, had his initial encounter with the Iban pirates, whom he called Sea Dayaks, and with whom he had his most dramatic confrontation. After the middle of the nineteenth century this heartland was to be the most loyal Iban area of all Brooke's domains.

Before the Iban migrations these rivers were sparsely inhabited by small, sometimes nomadic tribes such as the Kantus, Bugaus, and Serus. The Ibans took over these lands and drove the natives out or subdued and enslaved them. The Bukitans, who had crossed into Sarawak from Kapuas some generations before the Ibans arrived, were more difficult to conquer. Some authorities credit the Bukitans with the first use of the term Iban to designate the invaders. Because the Bukitans put up a fight, the Ibans rather admired their spirit. Indeed, the story is told that when two leaders of the Ibans and Bukitans first met they fought fiercely with each other with blowpipes and spears. Neither being able to wound the other, eventually each inquired the other's name. When they discovered that they were both renowned chiefs of their respective tribes, and that they were closely related in that they worshiped a deity in common, the fairy goddess Kumang, they decided to become friends and allies. They cemented their partnership by the marriage of the Bukitan chief's son with the daughter of the Iban chief.

Even though, in the end, the Bukitans were brought to heel by the Ibans, many more Bukitans married into Iban longhouses and many others melted into Iban society as slaves or military allies, scouts, and guides.

The Ibans, however, were not the only enslavers of Bukitan people. The Kayans to the north had a practice by which they presented a Bukitan with an iron implement or tool, demanding in return a certain measure of paddy. If the Bukitan could not pay the right amount of rice, his children became the slaves of the Kayan.

In terms of historical time, the pioneering period lasted until about the beginning of the eighteenth century. During this phase settlements were made on all the important upland streams of the Second Division. But as yet the area was so vast in terms of virgin land for cultivation, and so sparsely inhabited, that little or no inter-Iban friction occurred.

For the time being there was land in plenty, and except for driving out small weak tribes, or absorbing them, or annihilating them, Iban energies were taken up in laying claim to lands, establishing longhouses, clearing virgin jungle, and growing hill rice.

Some of the leaders of small Iban bands who migrated and settled in those new lands established families which continued to maintain the headships of villages and longhouse communities and in time assumed the status of first families. A simple political structure thus emerged, revolving about leadership exerted by first families and their relationships with one another. The Iban aristocrat was in a position of political prestige first and foremost because of his leadership abilities, which might or might not include military prowess. Recent writers on present-day social structure have noted the existence of an upper class of Ibans, most of whom trace their lineage to first families of the pioneering period. In some villages upper-class Ibans occupy the central and larger *bilek*s (apartments) of the longhouse, while in others the longhouse may consist wholly of upper-class families related by blood, together with their retainers.

There is little doubt that the Ibans took possession of the upstream territory in the Second Division. Traditionally, the felling of virgin forest gave the farmer certain rights to the land. If, after a few seasons, he abandoned that land and moved on to other fields, he still claimed the rights to the plot, and his family habitually returned there, after the land had lain fallow for fifteen or twenty years, to cultivate it again for a few seasons. As population in the area increased, the pattern of land ownership naturally became extremely complex, and Ibans were compelled to move into new territories downstream. By the nineteenth century they had expanded from the Batang Lupar and Saribas into the watershed of the mighty Rajang.

Thus, even though the historic period of the pioneers ended at about the beginning of the eighteenth century, the pioneering process of expansion and settlement into new lands, especially into the Rajang area and northward, continued throughout the nineteenth century. In economic terms a pioneer area is one in which some clearing and cultivating of primary jungle takes place. Inasmuch as there were no Ibans living north of the southern tributaries of the Rajang at the beginning of the nineteenth century, and in the present century two-thirds of the Iban population lives along the Rajang and its tributaries, the pioneering process of expansion constitutes a very large portion of Iban history, continuing right up to the present day.

In the process of expansion and settlement, friction and rivalries developed among the Ibans, and these disputes were aggravated by the complexities of the land system. By tradition, Ibans practiced a sometimes brutal but nevertheless effective way of settling land disputes. The Dayaks of two communities which claimed the same lands came together armed with sticks and began beating each other. Some warriors kept especially strong and effective clubs, studded with barbs and knobs, for these land wars. The longhouse community that prevailed took title to the disputed tract. During the Brooke period a clever outstation officer reportedly persuaded the Dayaks involved in one such land dispute to substitute a more friendly competition in the form of a cockfight. And the Dayaks seemed quite happy with the solution thus obtained.

Eventually land possession was claimed by the decision of chiefs or leading families. The second white rajah, Charles Brooke, was to decree that no one could possess land in any river drainage other than the one in which he lived. But in the meantime two things led to a long period of inter-Iban strife. The first was the pressure of new people from the continuing migrations from the south into the area of the upper Batang Lupar and Saribas. And the second was the seminomadic character of the Ibans, ever in search of new rice lands.

While conflicting claims to rice lands and feuds between longhouses formed a part of the inter-Iban friction, much of the unrest centered upon raids of Ibans from the Kapuas area into the Sarawak Iban villages and counterraids by Sarawak Ibans. Such headhunting and marauding expeditions were endemic in the remote interior well into the present century, and aggravated the problems of the Brooke government in its attempts to pacify the tribes.

But before this phase of the Ibans' story was acted out, there unfolded another more devastating and bloody period of conflict and unrest which involved the Ibans with the coastal Malays and with the white European intruders.

While Ibans were beginning their expansion over the hills from the Kapuas watershed into the headwaters of the Batang Lupar, some of the coastal people of northwest Borneo were embracing the Moslem faith. Islam spread by means of the trade and influence of Malacca. Brunei was a Moslem sultanate late in the fifteenth century. Some of the other river tribes adopted Islam, among them the Lugus people of the lower Saribas. Thus the Lugus became 'Malays,' and the present Malay population of Saribas is descended from this ancient tribe.

When the Ibans first encountered the Malays as they penetrated into the lower waters of the Batang Lupar and Saribas, they called them *orang laut*, men of the sea, because they came from the direction of the sea. While the first contacts between Malays and Ibans roused nothing more than curiosity, the encounter was to prove fateful for both peoples. On the one hand the Ibans were settling the upper river valleys and uplands of Sarawak, while on the other the Malays, under semi-independent chiefs who controlled the river mouth, were claiming political hegemony of the whole of the northwest coastal region under the general suzerainty of the Sultan of Brunei. The Ibans were to become enemies of some of the Malays and allies of others.

The rivers of Borneo have largely governed economics and politics. The ability of a leader or a tribe to enforce the payment of tribute or tax in kind—usually rice—along a stretch of river or coast has traditionally been the measure of the political state. Riverine and coastal states built on this form of power proliferated in Southeast Asia. Conversely, the inability of a chief to collect rice was the measure of 'independence' of a village or a river area. It was a rule of thumb in Borneo that the more remote the village in the upper reaches of the river, the greater was its 'independence.' Only in the present century has a central authority downriver or on the coast been able to reach the remote interior villages and rivers with its administrative apparatus and bureaucratic controls with any degree of certainty or regularity.

As Brunei extended its authority over the coast, the task of collecting tribute was left to the vassal Malay chiefs who controlled the river mouths and the lower reaches. Some of these Malay chiefs were descended from Minangkabau immigrants who came from Sumatra, perhaps after the Ibans had begun their upriver settlements. The Sultan of Brunei decreed an annual door or *bilek* tax of one *pasu* of rice (about a bushel) from Iban as well as Malay families. According to the ancient manner of tax collecting—which must have been close to universal habit, so widespread was it in early societies—the collector retained a portion of the tax as his fee or salary. The tax collector, of course, collected as much as he could, and in whatever way seemed best to him, in excess of the stated *pasu* of rice. Even at the best of times the Ibans resented the Malay taxman; and the taxman's trickery hardly improved the situation. One of the more common devices used by the collectors was an expanding basket which stretched when filled to hold more than one *pasu*. Another was a collection basket with a false bottom in which rice in excess of the tax was secreted.

The resentment against the presumption of Malay Brunei to rule over Iban longhouses and against the perfidy of Malay taxmen extended to include whole Malay communities in the coastal region just because they were Malays and gave the aggressive Ibans an excuse to attack Malay villages. For the Ibans, a Malay enemy head was quite as valuable a prize as the head of an Iban or other tribal enemy. In many ways fighting the Malays was more rewarding so far as prestige was concerned, for the Malays represented a more formidable enemy and a more sophisticated people than the weak tribes of the upper river regions. Iban-Malay warfare, however, was patchy. In Saribas there developed a tacit understanding between Malay and Iban that land upstream from the mouth of the Paku tributary was Sea Dayak territory and land down-river toward the coast was Malay. Some Ibans began to use Malay titles such as Orang Kaya (rich man) and Temenggong (chief).

Eventually Malay river chiefs were to turn the marauding energy of the Ibans to their own advantage. For there came a time when many Malay chiefs found that the collection of the rice tax for Brunei from the discontented Ibans was much less rewarding than the occupation of piracy, and of course much less exciting.

Brunei in its day had been a powerful state, capable at its height of demanding and receiving tribute payments from Manila, the coasts of Mindanao, and the Sulu Islands, as well as the coastal regions of Borneo. Its political power stemmed from its ability not only to exact tribute but to control the commercial traffic along the coasts and up the rivers. The Moslem Malay chiefs were its instruments of control, and the power of the Brunei sultans depended on their ability to hold the loyalty of these river chiefs.

By the middle of the eighteenth century the decline of Brunei was apparent. Some authorities attribute this decline to the disruption of the commercial economy (on which political power rested) by the Portuguese, the Dutch, and other Europeans who, from the sixteenth century onward, came more and more to dominate the commercial scene. Undoubtedly a partial reason for the decay lay in the natural tendency of states that have achieved a high level of prosperity and sophistication to succumb to luxury, high living, poor leadership, and internal corruption. The Brunei rulers' loss of control over outlying parts of the sultanate and the falling away of the Malay chiefs into a semiautonomous condition were accompanied by a change in occupation from tax collecting to tribute collection by extortion and marauding. From commerce to piracy was a natural step, for if the chiefs could no longer make a satisfactory livelihood by peaceful trade and collection, they could do so by force.

While probably not all the Malay chiefs indulged in commercial piracy or practiced extreme extortion among the villages, many of the chiefs along the northwest coast of Borneo took up the profession, and many others, including the rajahs and sultans of Brunei and Sulu, condoned and at times connived at the practice. Sulu and Brunei, by the beginning of the nineteenth century, were great marts where the booty of pirate expeditions was divided up and disposed of and where captives were sold as slaves.

The chiefs of the Saribas, Batang Lupar, and Skrang rivers of Sarawak were particularly energetic marauders. These Malays were not slow in recruiting the war-loving, headhunting Ibans to their service as warriors. Their expeditions ranged up and down the coasts of Borneo and into adjacent seas, and their victims were small villages and weak tribes, such as Melanaus and Land Dayaks, and small vessels of the coastal and island trade in the area. The partnership of Malays and Ibans proved a successful and lucrative arrangement. The Ibans were quite happy with this warring life, which provided a plentiful supply of head trophies, while the Malays profited from the plunder and the sale of slaves. The Malays, with their Iban allies, were second in ferocity among Southeast Asian pirates only to the Illanun and Balignini seafaring warriors, who were perhaps the most feared. These people, who were based in and around Mindanao and Sulu, made long pirate voyages in oceangoing boats of up to one hundred tons equipped with cannon, banks of oars, and fifty- or sixty-man crews. They moved in fleets of up to a hundred boats around the entire coastline of Borneo, pouncing on their prey among the islands south of Singapore and those of the South China Sea off the southwest tip of Borneo.

The Ibans came in contact with Illanun raiders when these fierce sea rovers invaded the Saribas and other Borneo rivers to plunder Malay and Iban villages alike. Many prestigious Illanun heads accrued from these encounters.

While the Illanun and Balignini would attack any trading vessel wherever encountered, the Malays and Ibans concentrated their at-tacks on coastal villages and on small native traders caught on the reefs and sandbars or becalmed along the coast, seldom venturing out of sight of land.

With or without allies, the Ibans were the pirates of the coasts of the Second and Third divisions and as far south as Pontianak in Dutch Borneo as early as the end of the eighteenth century. Europeans who ventured into the area and knew of these seagoing warriors labeled them Sea Dayaks, and during the succeeding half century or so the Sea Dayaks' reputation for piracy branded them as enemies to trade and commerce in the region. "They are," said one nineteenth-century account, "robbers by land and pirates by sea; their hand is against every man and every man's hand is against them." It was this feature of Iban activity which dominated the Western mind, and not the basic migratory and agricultural habits of the people. Indeed, it was only later in the nineteenth century that the English and Dutch, who ventured up the Borneo rivers at some personal risk, learned enough about the Ibans to realize that sea roving and piracy were fairly late developments.

It is quite probable that the prevalence of piracy on the coasts of Borneo, coupled with the European traders' desire to explore for themselves the trading potential of the rivers of Borneo, led to the initial political and naval intrusion of the British on the northwest coast. James Brooke was not the first Englishman to interest himself in Borneo. In earlier centuries servants of the great United East India Company had sailed the northwest coast seeking trade. Among them Alexander Dalrymple in the 1760's arranged for a company factory on Balembangan Island off the northern tip of Borneo, and company ships had occasionally taken on pepper and beeswax and birds' nests at Brunei for the China trade.

By tacit understanding, later confirmed by treaties, the Netherlands and Britain divided Borneo between them in the nineteenth century. Dutch Borneo became a part of the East Indies empire ruled from Batavia (now Djakarta). British Borneo had a more checkered colonial history. From mid-century the northwest coast was considered a British sphere, and indeed Britain acquired a crown colony there, the island of Labuan, as early as 1846. But not one of the three states of Sarawak, Brunei, and North Borneo became a British colony until the end of World War II. From 1841, Sarawak was the domain of the English rajah James Brooke and his successors for a hundred years. Brunei has always been an independent Moslem Malay sultanate, with strong treaty relations with Britain dating from 1847. North Borneo, formerly a part of the Brunei sultanate, was acquired by a British commercial company in 1878 and, with a charter from the crown, was administered as an independent state by a court of directors sitting in Old Broad Street in the City of London.

All three states were granted the intermediate status of proctectorate in 1888. And while Brunei remains under that designation to the present time, North Borneo and Sarawak became crown colonies in 1946 and seventeen years later joined in the Federation of Malaysia.

When Brooke anchored his yacht *Royalist* in the Sarawak River in August 1839, his meeting with the inhabitants initiated a new period for that part of Borneo, and his coming was to have a special impact upon the Iban society of the Saribas, Batang Lupar, Skrang, and Rajang rivers.

James Brooke had entered the East India Company service as an officer in a Bengal regiment. He was wounded before Rangoon during the first Anglo-Burmese war in 1825 and returned to England. Some biographers say that the wound left him impotent, and certainly Brooke never married. Yet others relate that during his long convalescence in Bath he had a love affair with a housemaid. In any event, years later, on one of his infrequent visits to England he was introduced to, and acknowledged, a natural son, much to the embarrassment of friends and family, especially of his brother-in-law the Reverend Charles Johnson who was rector of White Lackington, Somerset, and father of James Brooke's heir Charles Johnson Brooke (who later became the second rajah).

Very soon after his return to the East, Brooke resigned from the company service and in 1836, having inherited a respectable fortune, bought and equipped a schooner of 142 tons and set out to satisfy his sense of adventure and curiosity in the East Indies. His objective was to explore the coasts of Borneo and Celebes, but when he put into Singapore in May 1839, he was given a quasi-political mission as well. Singapore traders commissioned Brooke to carry a present to one of the Brunei rajahs who had shown himself to be somewhat above the general level of Brunei nobles by his kindness and help to shipwrecked English sailors. Rajah Muda Hasim was known to be in Sarawak, then the southernmost province of the Brunei sultanate. Thither Brooke went with present and letters of introduction to the rajahs and the Sultan of Brunei from Governor Bonham of Singapore.

When Brooke arrived, the political situation along the coast of Sarawak was chaotic. Malay and Iban piracy and marauding were merely part of this chaos. There was, too, the long-term resentment between Iban communities and their Brunei suzerain and the Malay river chiefs who practiced extortion to obtain tribute tax. On the Sarawak River, however, the conflict that prevailed was between a group of rebel Malay chiefs and the rajah of Brunei from whom they were attempting to wrest control. Rajah Muda Hasim, uncle of the sultan and chief minister of Brunei, was in Sarawak to suppress the rebellion. James Brooke involved himself in the civil war on the side of the Brunei rajahs, and his part in the proceedings forms one of the most romantic episodes in the pages of British colonial history. Brooke and Brunei prevailed, and for his part in aiding Brunei the sultan made over the government of Sarawak to Brooke. When the grant was confirmed in perpetuity Brooke found himself the first of a line of white rajahs who, for more than a century, ruled as Oriental potentates from a small palace in Kuching. In order of precedence in the British empire, the white rajahs of Sarawak ranked just below the maharajahs of India. As early as 1847, on his first visit back to England, Brooke was presented at court to Queen Victoria in Windsor Castle as Rajah of Sarawak.

Rajah Brooke was a romantic figure. He had a zest for adventure and at the same time felt drawn to the Malays and the peaceful Dayak peoples of Sarawak. His dream, stemming from the sense of order inherent in his character, was to stamp out lawlessness and the piratical activities of the Illanun, Malays, and Ibans and to establish peaceful British influence along the coasts of northern Borneo. Not much of an administrator and with little head for finance, he was at his best when leading attacks against Malay and Iban warriors. His relations with the people were warm and cordial, and he gained the loyalty and devotion of natives and Englishmen alike. Almost every evening he held open house for Malays and Dayaks who came for long evenings of talk with himself and his officers. Thus he kept himself informed of all that was happening in his kingdom. Later, he was to bemoan the fact that when his officials began bringing their wives to live in Sarawak the social evenings became more European and the natives stopped dropping in. Nevertheless he was among the Malays and Dayaks and Chinese daily, visiting their kampongs and shophouses and taking meals with longhouse dwellers. Not since the days of Stamford Raffles had the English in the Malay world found so heroic a figure to lead the way in imprinting on it the English way of peace and commerce.

Through the forties and fifties Brooke's intention to bring justice to the coasts and rivers was obstructed by pirates. The various political machinations of the Malay chiefs included stirring up trouble between downriver Ibans and the tribesmen upstream. By this means the Malay chiefs such as Indra Lila thought best to control both groups of Ibans and their territories. So Skrang and Saribas Ibans fought with the Ibans of Undop and Lingga and Batang Ai. They were, said the English explorer Earl, "engaged in perpetual warfare." He went on to observe that "the necessity of obtaining human heads to grace the marriage rites . . . tends strongly to check the increase of population, ..." Head-taking was the chief motivation of warfare. At the same time Malays and Ibans and Illanuns continued their coastal raiding.

In the six years between May 1843 and July 1849, Rajah Brooke led several naval expeditions against the Malays and Ibans of the Saribas, Batang Lupar, and Skrang areas and effectively put an end to their piratical forays. His method was to lie in wait for the pirate boats, surprise them and pursue them up the rivers to their hideouts. Fortifications along the way were destroyed, and finally the rebels' villages and longhouses were burned. Longhouses were burned in Paku and Rembas in the Saribas country and in Kanowit, a large tributary of the mighty Rajang River where Brooke came across a pirate lair that contained three hundred freshly taken heads.

After the greatest of all these forays to suppress Malay-Iban piracy, the battle of Batang Maru in July 1849, in which only eleven of ninety-eight pirate boats escaped destruction, most of the Ibans either submitted with pledges to loyalty to Brooke or disappeared into the interior. From then onward, British warships showed themselves at frequent intervals in the rivers and on the coasts to discourage any further outbreak of piracy. But these pirate battles almost lost Brooke his good reputation in England. He was accused by the Aborigines Protective Society and by no less a person than the future prime minister William Gladstone of slaughtering peaceful and innocent natives for his own greedy motives.

Stamping out coastal raiding with the aid of British naval squadrons was one thing: bringing an end to inter-Iban warfare in the interior was quite another. It was left to Sir Charles Brooke, the second white rajah, to tame the Ibans. In a short decade in Sarawak he came to be known as chief of all the Sea Dayaks and was so called by his uncle, the first rajah, to whom he was heir. Among the Dayaks, Charles was known as the Tuan Muda so long as his uncle ruled.

From his arrival in Sarawak as a cadet in his uncle's service in 1852 until he assumed the government in 1863, Charles Johnson Brooke lived and worked among the Dayaks of the Second Division, residing much of the time at Lingga on the Batang Lupar. Always a careful and thorough administrator, he gained the respect of the former Iban marauders by patience and a fair but practical administration of justice, following as closely as possible the customary codes of the villages. Unlike his uncle Rajah James, Charles was not renowned for his warmth of manner and feeling, but he was greatly respected for his fairness and discipline. For fifty years he ruled Sarawak, but it was during his first ten years while he was an outstation officer and while his uncle still ruled in Kuching that he formulated the principles and developed the practices that were to distinguish his later reign.

Charles's method of dealing with inter-Iban warfare was a rough and primitive form of jungle combat in which he used fiercely loyal Iban warriors of the lower rivers to subdue the restless interior peoples. Indeed much of the success of the Sarawak government in the pacification of the upriver Ibans was due to the Ibans' love of headhunting and warfare. Rajah Charles Brooke used this tribal custom in a strategy by which he was to suppress warfare among the interior tribes by leading punitive expeditions of Iban warriors recruited to his service. These expeditions became his chief instrument in the search for peace in the country. Brooke himself would lead his Ibans into remote offending villages, laying waste farms and burning longhouses. In this way the most recalcitrant had to submit or face being hounded to the farthest upland streams and mountains. In Brooke's army of Ibans, the reward for service was the heads of those rebels unwise enough to resist and unlucky enough to fall in the attack.

The underlying purpose of all this apparently aggressive action was to bring an end to inter-Iban strife, to create peace along the rivers, and to impose the rule of law. The problem faced then was that of extending the white rajah's legal and actual authority up the most remote streams, and of persuading Iban communities not only to accept Brooke law but to give up their seminomadic life in search of new farmland, and to settle down. The expansion of Brooke's authority during the 1840's and 1850's coincided with the beginning of the Iban migrations into the Rajang country and the vast region of the Third

Division, which Brooke annexed in 1861. The long effort to settle the Ibans extended well into the present century and represents part of the impact of modern capitalist life upon the longhouse dwellers. Meanwhile, throughout the reign of Rajah Charles, the punitive expedition remained the chief means of extending Brooke rule of law, and in this sense it partly resembled the former Malay method of extending Brunei's authority to tax. By recruiting lower-river Ibans to suppress upriver Ibans the white rajahs nourished the Iban love of war and head-taking, and these proclivities remained a lively part of life well into the twentieth century.

Not unnaturally, among peoples without writing but whose oral traditions were many, legend upon legend grew around the name and exploits of Rajah Charles. For the Ibans he became as much a legend as he was a man. His expeditions were unfailingly successful and he was fierce, persistent, and brave in extending the authority of Kuching, whether by storming the rebel Rentab's redoubt on Mount Sadok in the Skrang district or by admonishing his officers to get out among the Dayaks and administer government face to face with the natives. These and other methods of government were largely successful.

Rajah Charles wore a glass eye, the result of an accident while hunting in England. Evidently the eye fitted rather poorly, since he was forever losing it in the mud at river landing places or along jungle paths as he took his daily ride. He therefore kept a supply of 'tiger' eyes as the Dayaks called them. The lost eyes were sometimes found by Dayaks, who prized them as symbols of great luck and as proof that the eye of the great rajah was ever observing them. To the simple Dayaks, with whom he was always strict and just, Rajah Charles seemed to embody all the characteristics of the 'great white father.' Following the first rajah's example and his own early experience as an outstation officer, Charles established European residents at strategic points on the rivers of Sarawak, usually by the confluence of a tributary with the mainstream. There they lived close to the Dayaks, whom they administered with a simple and effective brand of justice, half-European, half-Dayak *adat* law. They heard cases in their palm-leaf roofed courthouses or in the open, meted out fines and punishment, collected the revenue from the longhouses, one dollar per *bilek* per annum, and generally kept in touch with conditions in their districts. The European residents were required to write up their every act in lengthy reports to the rajah in Kuching, for he insisted on knowing in minute detail the events in each district. Rajah Charles' rule was a very personal one, even to the extent of selecting the furnishings for the outstation residences and offices. There is a story that on one occasion, when an officer had requested an easy chair for his outstation quarters, the rajah refused it. The grounds for refusal were that if the officer was not touring his district or hearing cases, he should be at his desk writing reports or in bed sleeping and did not need an easy chair.

Not only was Rajah Charles's rule strict and despotic, but in his later years he could be petty and mean. He was in the habit of selecting the music for the Kuching Band to perform at their weekly concerts on the *padang,* or town square. On one occasion he dismissed the conductor because "the band was somewhat worse last evening, the programme was badly chosen, and I can't stand this any longer. . . ." Rajah Charles was invariably fair with his officers, but many of them feared his anger and would never think of being absent from a concert or leaving before the rajah made his departure. There was a strong feeling among them that their fortunes and status in the rajah's service depended upon close attention to such petty details of manners and conduct.

Then, too, the weekly dinners at the Astana were comically and uncomfortably formal affairs, the rajah usually insisting on singing, in uncertain key, his favorite Italian and French arias. But fortunately for the officers present he dismissed them with a curt good night at an early hour.

After the rebellious Rentab's defeat and self-exile to a longhouse by a remote stream in 1861, there was no great challenge from the Ibans to Brooke rule. Yet Brooke never really succeeded in curing the restlessness and bickering among the upriver Ibans, and the complex problems of administration involving these people were left for his son and successor, the third rajah, to sort out. Rajah Charles's despotic rule had been a highly individualistic one and his officers carried through his examples of direct face-to-face administration in the districts in the slower pace of the world of the nineteenth century. By the 1920's and the 1930's the outside world was beginning to impinge more and more upon Sarawak, and government in Kuching was becoming more bureaucratic. As a result, residents were confined more to their desks and their paperwork, and contact with the people in more remote areas tended to decrease. Rajah Charles Vyner Brooke, the third white rajah, was of a more aloof and remote character than his father, and the work of carrying on the personal style of rule of the second rajah had little appeal to him. This aspect of his character undoubtedly underlay the fact that the second rajah despaired of his older son, thinking him too much of a playboy and too deeply influenced by his wife's family, the Eshers, a type of English aristocrat for whom Rajah Charles had little admiration. Rajah Charles openly favored his second son Bertram Brooke, the Tuan Muda, but his sense of propriety dictated that the older son should succeed to the raj. In his will, however, Charles took the precaution of closely associating his second son with the government of his older son the third rajah.

Rajah Charles Vyner Brooke was prone to leave administrative detail to heads of departments. The result was a proliferation of regulations and paperwork at a time when the governing process was already becoming more complex, leaving administrators little time and energy for that 'getting out among the Dayaks' that characterized the practice of Rajah Charles's residents.

For the Ibans, the new style left something of a vacuum. The leadership to which they had become accustomed changed out of recognition. Some of the problems of governing the Ibans, such as what measures to take to obviate unrest caused by land disputes, were left over from Rajah Charles's day. The goal of the Kuching government was always to discover ways in which the Ibans could be assisted to improve their living conditions. To do this they had to be encouraged to stop their frequent migrations in search of land and to adopt settled agriculture. The government agricultural department advised diversification of crops and encouraged wet rice culture to wean the Ibans from their old dependence upon hill rice. Recalcitrant and rebellious villages were sometimes removed en masse from a remote area to a downriver area where the terrain made it possible to introduce them to wet rice agriculture.

In the first years of the twentieth century rubber planting was introduced. Chinese immigrants in lower river locations took to growing rubber as they had in an earlier time taken to pepper planting. But the Ibans were slower to adapt to this work and less careful and patient in tending rubber than were the Chinese. Some of them even believed that rubber trees were incompatible with their precious hill paddy spirits and drove them away. Surprising as it may seem, on the strength of this superstition the Ibans in some places began cutting down their rubber trees.

But diversification of farming by growing rubber and cassava and fruit trees was a fairly successful move to create an alternative source of income and to reduce reliance upon the vagaries of hill rice crops. The difficulties faced in introducing new crops were of a special kind. The rhythm of Iban life revolved about the hill paddy cycle and a belief in the governing spirits of the rice plant. So long as the Ibans clung to their tribal rice-spirit religion, the best that could be hoped for was to introduce crop diversification slowly. While some of their fellow tribesmen farther down the rivers took to settled agriculture based on wet rice cultivation, and while some others become urban dwellers, the upriver Ibans clung, and still cling, to their traditional ways, so that their problems of making a sufficient livelihood were, and still are, only partially relieved by crop diversification.

THE LONGHOUSE

The fact that the traditional mode of life in Sarawak among the Ibans and other Dayaks has not yet disappeared is to some extent the result of a century of rule by the white rajahs. We have already seen something of their unique role on the tropical island of Borneo. No one can dispute that, whatever the deficiencies of that century in which uncle, nephew, and grandnephew of the Brooke family pacified tribal Sarawak, the result before the eruption of World War II was a certain order and calm in the tangle of tribes and a certain harmony between them and their rulers, both in the capital at Kuching and in the interior where the white representatives lived and administered what they thought, often rightly, to be justice.

Long before the coming of the first Westerners, however, the peoples of Borneo had been working out their own destinies in their own peculiar ways. Among the Ibans, and in different forms among other tribal groups in Borneo, the central visible symbol of their way of life is the longhouse. Considered as a social phenomenon, an expression of semicommunal living, considered even as architecture, the longhouse is interesting. A village under one roof is rare in the world— whether in developed or underdeveloped areas—but in Borneo even today it is the home in which the majority of Dayak people live.

In keeping with their open nature, the Ibans do not hide themselves away deep in the jungles. They are sociable, amiable people, fond of innocent fun, often witty as they grow older but seldom turning to bitterness of tongue. Their outlook is strongly conditioned by the physical environment of the jungles and rivers, the problems of earning a living from primitive agriculture, and the even more intricate problems of placating and pleasing the spirits that are everywhere and in everything.

For convenience, the Ibans like to live near rivers—because rivers form the easiest and often virtually the only practicable highways of Borneo. They are the communication lines between the longhouse communities and the outer world—the world by the sea coasts where towns and Chinese trading communities lie, and where tribesmen feel ill at ease. It is a touching sight in a little town that has perhaps only three or four main streets at most, and where the traffic is hardly overwhelming in volume, to watch a group of visiting country people hesitate on the sidewalk, looking with some bewilderment from side to side at approaching cars and cycles, quite unsure what would be the best moment to cross the road. Those sleepy little towns of Borneo are the farthest perimeter of the Iban world—at least for most of the longhouse dwellers.

An Iban village is built on a riverbank or not more than a five-minute walk from a river, close enough for easy access to their small boats, and for obtaining water, and for washing and bathing. Every village has one or two jetties—often mere split timbers on stilts in the shallows of the muddy water flowing by. Tied to the jetties there is usually a flotilla of *perahu*s, pelvis-wide dugout tree trunks shaped with great skill and infinite labor. Most of the *perahu*s are paddled, but these days the more prosperous communities are quite likely to own a few outboard motors which are fitted as necessity dictates to one or

A longhouse with its exterior platform on which stand a small perahu *and a Chinese storage jar. A notched log forms the stairway from the ground*

In former times the notched-log stairway to the longhouse was pulled up at night to keep enemies out

another of the *perahu*s. Even a fair-sized motor launch can sometimes be seen tied up to one of the makeshift Iban jetties.

The path from jetty to longhouse village is usually a slippery, muddy slope that may have been paved with small tree trunks or shafts of bamboo. But, as everywhere in Borneo where tropical rainfall is heavy, the mud oozes up and makes the going precarious. When the gradient is steep the logs are usually laid vertically up the slope, with notches cut into them to serve as steps. Even a handrail way be provided, especially when some important person is likely to call, a convenience that survives after his visit until it rots and falls down.

The longhouse village is a surprise, even if you have a rough idea of what to expect. Only one long building lies ahead, like some curious warehouse, in its clearing backed by the jungle trees. This odd type

of structure and its internal organization reflecting the pattern of Borneo Dayak life deserve some attention, in the same way that the skyscrapers of Manhattan would be a worthwhile subject for the visitor from some other planet who wanted to find out about an important aspect of American urban life. The longhouse is the context of Dayak village living.

The longhouse is perched on tall piles up to fifteen feet above the ground, and its entries are at either end. A good straight tree trunk slopes up from the ground to floor level, neatly notched with steps that are naturally more suited to bare feet than to visitors wearing shoes. One thing that strikes the visitor immediately, anywhere near a longhouse, is the noise. And on entering the doorway, one cause of the noise is at once evident--the floor. The traditional flooring of the

The ruai, *or communal area of the longhouse, where meetings are held and ceremonies take place*

longhouse is closely set bamboo poles not more than two or three inches in diameter. These are loosely held in position by cross straps at their ends, and the lightest footfall causes them to rattle. So in all but the more modern longhouses where planks have replaced the bamboos there is an almost continuous rattling of the floor.

The vista, as you enter, is surprising. The long corridor, open to a wide living area on one side and closed by a row of wooden doors on the other, is really the village main street, stretching right to the other end of the longhouse where another door acts as alternate entry or exit. The roof and side walls are supported by stout timbers, nowadays mostly of ironwood but formerly of big bamboos. And even now these are seldom nailed but are notched and lashed together without the use of metal. More prosperous longhouses are roofed with ironwood

shingles, while less well-off ones are thatched; and some recent structures present the depressing spectacle of a mixture of the traditional shingle or thatch with patches of rusty corrugated iron sheeting. Despite its basically sturdy construction, the longhouse generally gives the appearance of a ramshackle and makeshift building. We shall see later some reasons why this is so.

A big longhouse may contain up to sixty family apartments, but more often there are fewer. These apartments are called *bilek*s and stretch in a long row down one side, each separated from the next by a common wooden wall and from the interior of the building (from the village street, in fact) by its own door. All the families of the longhouse, therefore, dwell under one roof, and each family is responsible for maintaining that part of the roof over its own space. The *bilek* can

The Chinese jars in the bilek *are heirlooms. Magazine illustrations are a popular form of decoration*

be quite spacious and serves the family for eating, sleeping, and storing its possessions, among which are sometimes treasures in the shape of antique Chinese porcelain jars and brass gongs. A prosperous family may partition the *bilek* with board walls or curtains, making a large communal room and smaller areas that serve as cubicles for sleeping. These are often furnished with bedsteads or mattresses, and boxes where clothes are kept. But more often the bed spaces are merely small, low platforms against the walls or in corners. The main room is equipped with a crude fireplace against the outer longhouse wall, and above this is a hinged flap in the roof that can be raised to let out the smoke of the cooking fire or closed to exclude the heavy rain. Woven rattan mats are spread on the floor or on a slightly raised platform, and on these the family sits to eat or to talk. Modern *bilek*s

are quite likely to have a few wooden chairs and a table standing anachronistically about among crude pottery cooking pots and bamboo water pitchers.

Outside the row of *bilek*s runs the corridor (*ruai,* as it is named) which is the village street, although unlike most village streets it runs within the building and is therefore covered. Technically, the section of the *ruai* fronting each apartment belongs to the *bilek* owner and is generally where the husband's gaudy fighting cock is tied by a string; but it is used by all the longhouse population. Considered together with the larger area on the far side of the narrow street (also part of the *ruai*), it constitutes a very wide and extremely long covered area used for all manner of purposes from entertaining visitors to taking an occasional nap, from weaving rattan fishtraps to evening entertain-

Final winnowing and drying of rice, a tedious job generally lightened by laughter and joking

ment. The community life of the whole longhouse takes place there and the traffic back and forth is considerable, moving past and around and through whatever else is going on. In the *ruai* are stored and hung the farming implements and all manner of baskets. There, too, the women pound or husk the rice in large wooden mortars with hardwood poles used as pestles.

The tethered fighting cocks, periodically screeching at one another or just crowing for their own pleasure, are only one of the sources of noise in the longhouse. Prized possessions of the Ibans, men whose favorite pastime is cockfighting since headhunting is no longer allowed, these big aggressive birds strut to and fro the length of their tethers, pecking at the rice in cans beside them. One other noise-emitter of first caliber is the innumerable wandering dogs growling and barking both inside and outside the longhouse. No one takes any notice of these often mangy creatures, except children when the dogs are young enough to be cuddled. During predawn hours the fretful howls of these dogs are most troublesome—though apparently not to longhouse people, whose upbringing has inured them to almost any variety or degree of noise. There are also pigs, roaming and rootling under the house all day, the established scavengers of garbage and waste that falls through the slats of the floor above them. Despite the omnivorous nature of these pigs, the ground under and around most longhouses is generally an untidy morass of discarded objects of all kinds that even pigs cannot eat.

On the opposite side from the row of *bilek*s, and like them running the whole length of the building, is a kind of verandah or platform

Women and children filling their gourds. Most longhouses are near streams, their only source of water

To the right of the longhouse are kitchens, to the left a wide veranda

which is not under the roof but projects outward and stands on stilts like the longhouse itself. This *tanju* greatly increases the total floor area and is used for such activities as winnowing grain and for some of the more elaborate festival ceremonies.

Completing the available space is the area in the rafters of the longhouse used as storage space for farm implements and various baskets and matting not in daily use, and for the storage of rice in large dark boxes. Nowadays, however, the rice granaries are more often separate small huts raised on stilts and standing to one side of the longhouse. The stilts are usually fitted with large wooden or metal discs or flanges some way above the ground to discourage rats from climbing up and eating the grain. The attic or loft area inside the longhouse is sometimes partially floored, and on this upper level

the unmarried daughters may sleep, while the bachelors usually sleep on mats in the *ruai,* outside the *bilek.* As we shal. see later, this is a convenient arrangement in the context of Iban premarital relations and courtship.

Formerly longhouses were flimsy buildings, made to last at most for a few years, after which they were abandoned and the whole village moved to some other location. There they put up a new longhouse, sometimes using timbers from the old. This seminomadic life was dictated by the nature of the agriculture. Cultivating hill paddy (dry rice cultivation) by the slash and burn technique, in which the jungle and undergrowth are reduced to ashes and the ground planted, gives good crops for a few years, after which the yield falls dramatically, and a new area must be discovered where the same method is tried once

The nights are sometimes chilly enough for small fires. Among the hanging straws are smoke-blackened skulls

more. Hence the need to move every so often to another area nearer to new fields while the old ones lie fallow for up to twenty years. We will discover more about this ancient method of growing crops in a later chapter.

Perhaps the most peculiar aspect of the interior of the longhouse is visible only after you get used to the rather low light in the *ruai* area. From the beams and rafters hang clusters of human skulls. They are generally contained in wide-mesh nets and are in full view. Some of the skulls look quite recent, but most have a blackened, ancient look that reveals their age. Headhunting, a gruesome custom, was virtually eliminated long ago under the Brooke rule. But during the Japanese occupation of Borneo in World War II, the traditional Iban delight in the custom of taking heads was naturally not in any way discouraged, if the

heads happened to be Japanese. Thus, after years of suppression, the custom temporarily revived. And this explains the comparative freshness of some of the longhouse skulls.

Very often the skulls will be concentrated outside the *bilek* of the *tuai rumah*, the headman of the longhouse. An occasional longhouse even boasts a special head-house—a room often attached to the end of the main structure—in which ancient, graying skulls, dusty and encrusted with cobwebs and the nests of beetles and insects, are suspended in the same way as those elsewhere. Oddly enough, no special sanctity or religious significance attaches to this room, and it is treated much as any other storage space. The presence of human skulls in a longhouse today indicates the Ibans' liveliness of faith in the power of spiritual renewal that focused on human heads.

Mother and child

A family eating a meal by a stream. The longhouse dogs have accompanied them in the hope of pickings

Pigs under the banana trees at the foot of the notched-log stairway to a longhouse

The Ibans like to capture young hornbills and rear them as pets. This one is not yet adult

Iban children are much loved and petted, yet they are well-behaved and unspoiled

Father makes a fishtrap from split rattan as his children watch and learn

Building a new longhouse. When the community is wealthy, heavy belian *is used because of its resistance to termites*

Iban children are sometimes allowed to try the locally made cigarettes

Boys collecting the heavy jackfruits that grow in abundance in Sarawak

The boy on the right is rolling a cigarette. Both the bamboo and metal boxes contain tobacco and banana-leaf wrappings

Children make pets of cockerels that are kept tied by one leg outside the door of the bilek

Cockfighting is a favorite pastime of Iban men, and they bet heavily on fights

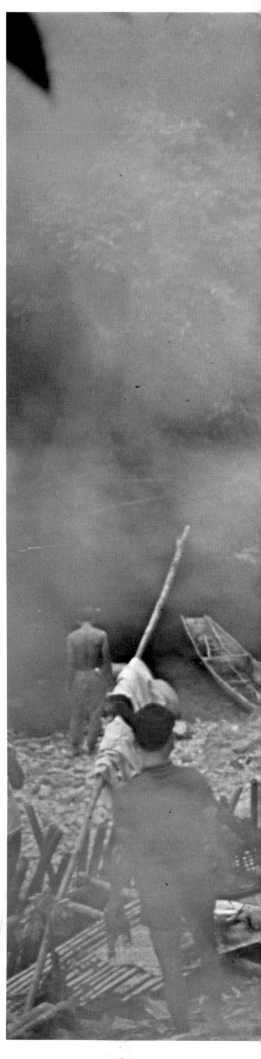

Preparing vegetables. The tattooing of women is very rare nowadays

In the making of rice beer, rice is cooked in bamboo logs

Young men dancing to the music of a two-string guitar called a sape

Rivers and streams are the jungle roads. This stream is bordered with ilipinut *trees*

Ibans are extremely fond of bathing and go to the river several times a day

Women fill bamboo logs with rice for making rice beer

Boats are loaded with purchases on a river near a small village market

Family lunch in the bilek. *Rice, eggs, vegetables, and morsels of fish or meat are salted at the meal*

There has been a great deal of scholarly controversy on the subject of headhunting. But the main significance of the custom seems to have been this concentration of what might be called the spiritual power that was thought to reside in the head of a victim. Originally the taking of heads had to do with the young Iban warrior's need to impress the young girls of the longhouse with his virility as displayed by his prowess in lopping off an adversary's head. It was, in other words, a kind of display of manhood. Its other aspect was that the heads themselves were thought to contain the spirit of the victim, and if the victim was an enemy, the Iban who took the head had the enemy's spirit in his hands. By extension of this idea the whole longhouse had captured something of the enemy's spiritual power, which thus became theirs in one form or another. The spirits of the animist Dayak world were pleased, placated, charmed, and rewarded for favors by presentation of fresh heads or, failing that, even of old heads.

Like most such tribal customs, headhunting was perhaps a rationalization of the impulse or the necessity to destroy enemies, or to eliminate neighboring tribal peoples who were a potential threat to the livelihood of the longhouse. By the time of the first Western reports from Borneo, headhunting had degenerated from its former ritualistic status into the extremely gruesome and horrible necessity to get heads at virtually any cost. A warrior who had no special enemy, or perhaps even not the courage or martial skill to lop off an enemy's head, would find out secretly where some corpse had been recently buried, then dig it up at night and take the head. One acting governor of the English colony of Labuan (an island just off the Borneo coast) buried his wife in a secret grave in his private garden, hoping to prevent Dayak head-snatchers from molesting the corpse.

What was once ritualistic and warrior prowess of a harsh but at least manly kind became a compulsion to acquire heads in whatever way they could be got. Even the heads of children who had strayed from some neighboring longhouse were perfectly acceptable; and so were the heads of unwary old ladies gathering leaves or berries in the jungle. So it is not surprising that the custom came in for severe repressive measures as soon as some form of administrative order was established in Sarawak by the Brookes.

Such is the average longhouse—a row of apartments with a common front yard, perched on stilts near a river and close to the fields from which all its inhabitants gain their living.

LIFE AND LOVE

The Ibans are a friendly people. Their innate feeling that they must be self-reliant and independent does not in any way conflict with a natural gregariousness and a lively pleasure in strangers. They welcome visitors, and their boisterous hospitality is unstinted. Unfortunately in past times, and even in the present, not all visitors to the longhouses have been as genuine as the hospitality offered, and it is best, whoever you may be, to give a little warning of a visit. This gives everyone time to consider what sort of guest is coming. Long experience of Chinese and European outsiders has tended to make the Ibans rather wary, for not all of these people have come with entirely friendly motives. The Ibans are sensitive about their dignity—and have every reason to be so. While they are a happy, singing, dancing, and tremendously frolicsome people, the peculiar forms of privacy and the definite proprieties of life in the longhouse are serious matters, seriously observed. The members of the community could hardly live so much in one another's pockets if these aspects of life were not properly regulated by a definite code of behavior.

Most Ibans are of medium height. Upcountry it is rare to find many of them taller than five feet three inches, although the town-dwelling few who have adopted a partly Western diet with a higher protein content readily grow two or three inches taller than that. The average Iban man is more ruggedly built than his Malay counterpart. He is smooth-skinned, and his coloration is in general a little darker than that of the other Dayak peoples, varying from a cinnamon yellow-brown to light tan. Iban hair is usually straight and very black, but there are heads of wavy hair to be found, and there is occasionally even a curly head. Any other color, it may be suspected, is the result of some European admixture in the not too distant past. It was not uncommon in the Brooke days for European resident district officers to take temporary 'wives' and father litters of brown-haired children. Iban men traditionally cut their hair in a characteristic way—the head being shaved some distance up from the brow and the hair allowed to fall forward in a fringe cut straight across the forehead, while the hair at the back was allowed to grow quite long. This gave the young men a slightly girlish look quickly belied by their manner and made the old men look curiously epicene. But nowadays this hairstyle is less common than formerly—but perhaps with the spread of the Western cult of hair, the old style, with modifications, will come into its own again, for it was generally becoming to the young.

A high proportion of Iban men are handsome, and an equally high proportion of the women are comely. They tend to be narrow in the hips and generally not of a buxom build, and they have a grace of appearance and movement. There is a rounded softness about them, and their features are in fine proportion to the smallish stature.

The children, like most children in Southeast Asia, hardly ever seem sad or morose. There is perhaps something about the Southeast Asian attitude to children, combined with the adventure playground type of surroundings many of them enjoy, that makes children happy and forever smiling. They fall asleep readily, amuse themselves just as easily, and are looked after most of the time by a grandparent. Fathers, especially, seem fond of their children, and it is a common sight in the *ruai* of the longhouse to see several fathers in conversation, sitting in a huddle on the floor, each cradling his favorite child.

Many older men have pierced earlobes in which heavy earrings used to be worn, giving them the look of long-eared Buddhas. The weight of the earrings gradually enlarged the hole in the lobe until a loop of pale flesh hung two or more inches downward from the bottom of the ear. Since some of the brass earrings weigh a quarter of a pound or so, when the men get drunk on the local alcohol of an evening, and especially when there is some festivity or there are visitors to entertain, their wives tend to remove the ornaments. Otherwise a violent shake of the head can damage the face as the earrings swing like pendulums against teeth or skull. But the wearing of earrings is less common today than it was.

The traditional clothing of the Iban men, young and old, is a loin-cloth—a length of brightly colored material about eighteen inches wide; the more festive the occasion, the brighter the color. This cloth is wound around the waist, brought between the legs, and tucked under the waistband in front, forming a small apron. When going on a journey, a short shirt or jacket is worn. The simplicity of this clothing assorts well with the humid heat of Borneo and allows freedom of movement in the jungle, on the river, and in the fields. While working on the farm the Ibans wear a conical hat of woven rattan or rice straw that is not unlike the 'coolie' hats of South China and may well have been adopted from Chinese immigrants. But the Borneo variety—or varieties, for there are many—is often intricately patterned with designs in various colors and is a thing of beauty in itself.

In recent years Iban men have begun to adopt the Chinese Southeast Asian working 'uniform'—a pair of cotton shorts and a tee shirt—and Iban women have taken to wearing brassieres and to having their hair curled at the Chinese beauty salons in the riverside markets. The result is aesthetically unpleasing not only for admirers of the semi-naked female form but by any standard one may care to apply. The brassiere was not designed as an exterior garment and its generally plain pale color looks ludicrous with the riotous hues of the sarong. In Sarawak it seems not to have been a question of missionaries or governments 'putting pants on the natives' but of a certain Dayak prudishness developing of its own accord under the influence of Western dress as seen in old magazines and the occasional movie. If proof is needed, you can find in almost every longhouse nowadays pages of pinups, a washed-out print of Her Majesty the Queen of England, and pictures of fading film stars pasted on the walls here and there.

As for the young men who have ventured far down the river to the towns and even, perhaps, made a trip to Singapore 400 miles distant over the sea, they return looking (to non-Iban eyes at least) extremely out of place in the longhouse. Teenage Western fashions in the less expensive range tend to be extreme, and young Ibans, with a natural love of adornment, buy the brightest and what they consider the best that they can afford. Their return home is greeted with celebrations in which they take part wearing their Western jacket and trousers, often a necktie, hot and uncomfortable shoes, and an air of tremendous sophistication. Alas, this new-found glamor soon wears off, for the buttons fall from the smart shirt, the trousers soon get ruined from sitting on the rough floor, and the joys of wearing a tie and shoes in the jungle prove less rewarding than the comfort of bare feet and an unencumbered body.

Nonetheless, the urge to wander far afield is strong in Iban men. There is an element of desire for financial gain in it when they go to the coastal towns and to the oilfields of Brunei, Sarawak's tiny neighboring

A cockfighting enthusiast with his bird. In his hat are the tail feathers of a hornbill

state. But much more than that, it seems that wandering is in a sense a substitute for the traditional warrior activities of headhunting and the like. Considerable prestige accrues to the Iban who spends a year or even just a few months far away from his longhouse. The money he brings back is welcome, but he himself is even more welcome in the hearts of the longhouse family. And his prestige ever after tends to be slightly higher than that of his fellows who have not seen the great outside world and managed to cope with it successfully. He has performed in Iban eyes the equivalent of the exploits of the warrior of old who went on a marauding expedition and returned with a string of fresh heads dangling from his loincloth.

A festival in the longhouse transforms the whole interior, much as some gala ball transforms the public rooms of a hotel in the West, and at such times the Ibans put on all their finery. The men dress up in their most colorful clothes, the usual loincloth supplemented by a short coat of goat or monkey fur decorated with the brightest feathers from local birds. Jangling silver and copper bracelets circle their wrists, upper arms, and legs, and various metal ornaments hang from the ears. Numerous long striped feathers of the sacred hornbill (*kenyalang*) are fixed in an embroidered cap or headdress, while strings of beads tangle around the men's necks in just the way that is now acceptable in the West. In the dancing and party games that accompany each festival, the costume is completed by a short straight sword, often in a decorated sheath, or a spear and an oval-shaped, patterned shield of wood. The whole effect is striking and virile, but not fearsome.

The girls also put on their best sarongs, often handwoven in fine

A young couple being married in their finery. They are blessed by the headman of the longhouse

patterns, and around the waist go several silver belts of intricate filigree work with various pendants such as old silver coins dangling from them. (Numbers of the ubiquitous Maria Theresa dollars have found a homes in Iban longhouses.) The girls often have elaborate necklaces of beads in the form of a loosely woven net draped over shoulders and breasts, and a headdress attached to the chignon completes the picture. In the days when this was the complete costume, the girls were a very fine sight indeed.

There is yet another feature of Iban adornment, perhaps even more distinctive than their clothes—tattooing. When and why tattooing began among the Dayaks of Borneo is unknown. With the Kayans the tattoo takes highly imaginative forms with animist overtones, each design having a symbolic content or representing an extremely stylized mystical figure or omen. The Ibans seem largely to have borrowed their decorative tattoo motives from other tribal peoples of Sarawak, and there is no strict rule about which design goes on this or that area of the body. The tattoos are therefore almost purely decorative in intent. Both men and women are decorated in this way—and there are certain designs peculiar to women, who usually prefer one or two small patterns on the breasts and the calves of their legs. But there is at least one old lady known who had many dots tattooed on her hands, and these, she said, were the method by which she kept score of her premarital affairs in the days of her youth! Contemplating these records must have conjured up pleasant memories for her of many a romantic evening long ago. The Ibans, as we shall see, are quite frank in these matters.

In those not so distant days, Iban youths were literally covered

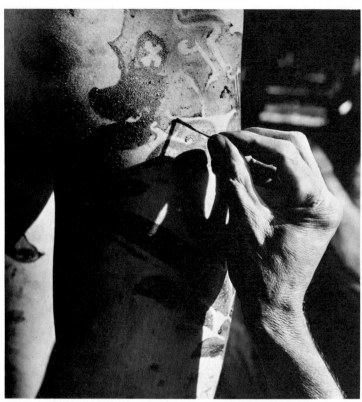

The stencil for a tattoo being painted with lampblack

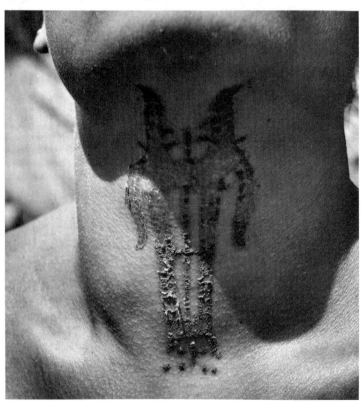

The throat tattoo is the most painful to have done

with tattooed designs according to whim—here a rosette, there some curvilinear motif, a dog, or a scorpion, and many others.

Tattooing is a long and painful process in Sarawak. A design is traced on the skin in black dye made from soot scraped from the bottom of a cooking pot and mixed with sweetened water. The longhouse tattooist then takes his small hammer and sharpened bamboo stick and with light taps on the stick punctures the skin in the area of the dye. The dark pigment penetrates the skin and spreads a little to join with that from the adjacent punctures. Because conditions during the whole operation are always less than aseptic, the fresh tattoo very often becomes infected and it is not an uncommon sight to see an Iban wearing not so much a tattoo as a scar inflicted unconsciously by the artist. For this reason, and also because of more frequent contacts

with the outside world where tattooing confers no special prestige, the practice is gradually going out of vogue.

The longhouse itself, as we have seen already, was and to some extent still is a temporary structure. Apart from the exigencies of shifting agriculture, there were other reasons why a move from the old to a new house was made, one of which was an outbreak of smallpox. Although it has now been controlled, the disease used to be a frequent scourge among upriver Dayaks. The old longhouse in this instance would be abandoned and left as a cemetery for the victims who had died. Another reason for rebuilding was consistently bad omens in the guise of the cries of birds or the frequent visitations of certain large birds.

The Iban *bilek* family is a supremely independent unit, and may opt, if it wishes, to move from one longhouse village and join another.

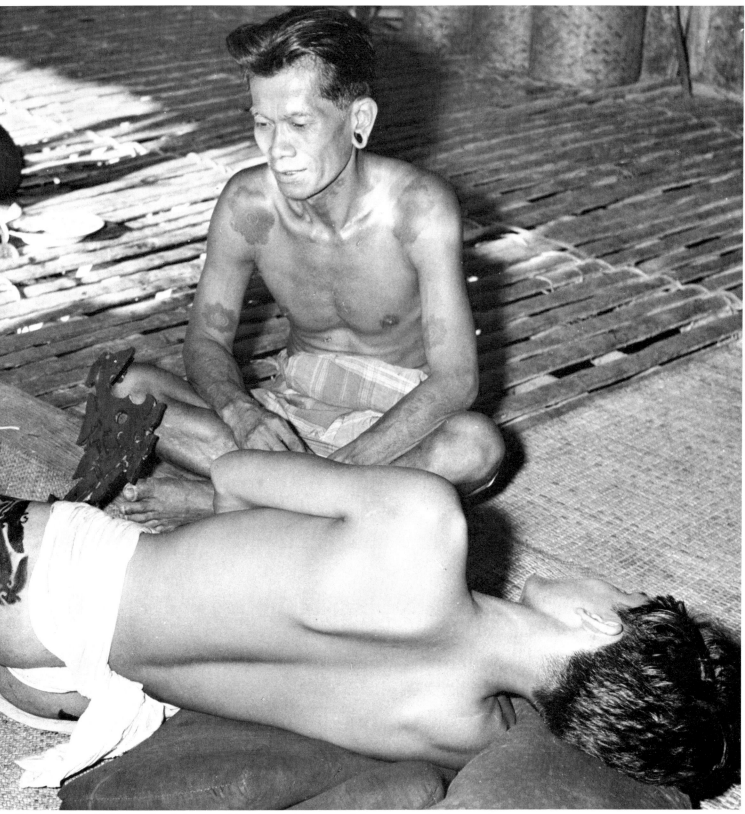

The tattooist with his needle of sharpened bamboo and hammer of the same material at work on a young man

The many families inhabiting the building live and work together in comparative harmony and organize life and work in a practical manner, but there is little property held in common. Nor, strangely enough, do there seem to be many bonds that unite the families, other than those which dictate this practical and convenient way of life and the general well-being of the community. The longhouse has, rightly, been called not so much a house of many rooms as a terrace of individual dwellings.

The Iban community is perhaps one of the least complicated societies of its kind. There are, of course, certain people who have authority, such as the *tuai burong*—'bird watcher' would be a rough translation of the words—who is a kind of guardian of the rituals and whose job it is to keep track of the proper ceremonies to be performed at certain times. His is the onus of reminding the inmates of the longhouse of ritual observances and of reading omens, and for this reason he is held in considerable respect. The *tuai burong* is generally but not invariably an elderly man, but he is not in any sense a priest. He acts more as a wise man in everything pertaining to the rice cycle and its rites and other similar matters. There is also a *tuai rumah*, 'guardian of the house, whose functions are rather like those of a civil official. He adjudicates in disputes between individuals or families and is also an expert on customs (collectively called *adat* law)

These two positions are not necessarily hereditary—each longhouse community electing the headmen of its choice—but by custom the jobs are frequently passed on to son or son-in-law or another male relative if everyone agrees that the candidate has the necessary qualities of wisdom, expertise, and leadership. Formerly, it was generally a leader

A girl from the upper Rajang River wearing an elaborate ceremonial headdress of beads

in warlike activities who was chosen, and at that time the *tuai rumah* might well occupy both positions. It was usual for the headman to elect a leading young warrior to succeed him when the time came.

It is tempting to think of the longhouse community as a nicely integrated group of families related by ties of blood and to leave it at that. While this is perfectly true, the organization and structure of society in the longhouse is not at all what such a statement would imply in a similar community elsewhere. It is, in fact, both curious and interesting. There is a definite tendency for young men and girls to marry within the longhouse community and there is no barrier to first-cousin marriage. But there is nothing to stop a young Iban from courting and marrying a girl from some other longhouse. It is generally only convenience, and doubtless propinquity, that make for marriages within the

community. There is a mild degree of social stratification in the Iban community. In the old days the precedence of 'first families' was observed, and descendants of those 'aristocrats' are still looked on as upper-class Ibans. But the distinction is not great, and there has never been any real rigidity or lack of mobility among those vague classes. In historical times anyone could marry upward, and movement in the classes seems generally to be in that direction. In marrying upward the family is assured of the higher social status of the family into which its offspring marries.

In courtship and marriage the Iban community is wide open. Free association is the norm, and nowhere is this more obvious than in relationship between the young. While marriage partners are often chosen by the parents, or at least approved by them, it is rather uncommon for

Men watching a regatta at Kapit. One has a traditional and the other a Western hairstyle

young people to be forced to marry against their will. The initiative is generally taken by the boy, who shows his serious intentions in various ways. But the girl of his choice is free to reject him without giving any special reason, and by custom her wishes have to be respected. If the rejected boy persists, he may very well be faced with the anger of the girl's brothers and other male relatives.

A decade or two ago in the West, the freedom of premarital relations between Iban youths and girls might have seemed more surprising than it does now in the context of our current 'permissive' society. There is in fact nothing permissive about Iban thought or attitude on the subject, which is codified by ancient tradition and conforms to perfectly sober Iban morals. Unlike many a Western or other Oriental community, the Ibans do not regard premarital sexual relations

as immoral, provided the matter is arranged according to the set patterns of their own custom.

When the parents of a sixteen-year-old girl find that she has begun to entertain a young man in her bed at night, they are neither surprised nor displeased. Their reaction is probably like that of Western parents who discover (or are told by the girl) that their daughter is dating Harry who is the son of family friends. At first, sexual relations may not in fact take place, and even if they do, should the boy be in any way displeasing to the girl, he is not invited again. On the other hand, if he has taken the initiative himself and made the overtures, it is not at all uncommon, should the girl not want him as a suitor, for him to be asked vociferously to leave. On such occasions he may well be helped on his way by the men of the girl's household. And a good deal of half-

Returning from bathing in the river

Bathing the baby in the shallows

Making a casting net

humorous, half-serious criticism is leveled at him for being presumptuous.

Once a boy and girl have passed four or five nights together, it is generally accepted in the longhouse that the boy has serious intentions. There is little apprehension about pregnancies occurring as a result of this nocturnal courtship. First, Ibans believe that intercourse must take place at least three times before conception occurs. And second, illegitimate birth is not frowned on so long as the boy comes from what the Ibans consider to be good stock. Quite commonly young men father several children on several girls before settling down with a permanent partner. The children are looked after by means of a payment agreed on with the mother and her family, and both parties are then free to go their separate ways. No one is surprised or injured or upset. In such matters the word of the *tuai rumah* is both helpful and final.

In this way the young Ibans get to know one another before they decide whom to marry. If we require to find some sort of a parallel in our own society, we need only recall the practice of 'bundling' in the North American frontier community, or the same sort of arrangement that still took place well into the twentieth century in the remoter areas of Scotland under the same name. The Iban manner of courting ensures a certain privacy for the young couple—something not easily come by in the noisy and crowded longhouse in daylight hours, when both the *ruai* and the *bilek* are almost continuously occupied by members of the family group. It also provides a sense of adventure and exploration for the young. There is little else in the way of entertainment that they can

Weaving a cotton blanket. The threads of the warp have been previously tied and dyed

arrange for themselves. Unconsciously, and in a very natural and healthy way, relationships between various young people are formed on a basis of knowledge and not just romanticism. On both sides there is the possibility of adequate experiment in lovemaking, and the result is that Iban boys and girls come to marriage well equipped by experience of one of its important aspects and with the likelihood of having chosen their partners wisely. Divorce, while not unknown, is relatively uncommon in the longhouse.

The Ibans are monogamous. In recent years Christian missionaries have tried to make them moral, in the Western Christian sense, as well. In some instances the missionaries have induced a change in the method, if not the pattern, of courtship. Some Iban families have been persuaded to abandon the habit by which the boy visits his girlfriend

in her boudoir, and instead the lad will sit talking with the girl in her family *bilek*, perhaps in the presence of the family. Marriages are arranged through such courting habits. Families who have thus been Christianized will sometimes testify loudly to their conversion to this courting practice when talking with outsiders or Europeans. They feel that this is the more 'sophisticated' way. But many *bilek* members will privately tell quite a different tale. The old custom dies hard, and Christianity, like other formal religions implanted in Southeast Asia, makes a rather superficial impression on pagan tribal peoples.

Iban girls apparently have little feeling against marriage with Malays, Chinese, or Europeans. Indeed it was very common for Chinese immigrant farmers in Sarawak to marry Iban wives and raise healthy and handsome families. The Iban young may even think of marriage

Mothers in conversation

A digger carrying a sack of guano from the deposits in the Niah Caves

A district officer of the government on patrol with his assistants

to a Chinese or European as enhancing their social status, for these latter are thought of as more sophisticated and worldly. Parents may object to such mixed marriages, but it may be for no better reason than an economic one—because the marriage of a daughter to a Chinese or European means that she will be lost to the family as a working member on the farm. For she will undoubtedly go to the town to live with her foreign husband in a completely different social environment. For the same reason parents may well disapprove of a daughter's marriage into another longhouse. In any event, the wishes of the girl usually prevail and parental prohibition is seldom pressed to an unhappy end.

There is a story told by the former British High Commissioner to Sarawak, Malcolm MacDonald, of the beautiful daughter of a headman who went away to the town downriver to school and fell in love there

with a young and handsome Chinese businessman, much against the will of her doting parents. Not receiving the blessings of her father upon her intended marriage to the youth, the girl returned sullenly to the longhouse. Soon the chief was busily planning his daughter's marriage to a respected Iban schoolteacher. But the girl had a mind of her own and meanwhile had secretly made a liason with another young man, with whom she was presumably in love. In good time the young pair slipped away together to a distant place far up a tributary stream and there lived together in a rough jungle hut for the five days and nights prescribed by Iban custom to constitute a recognized marriage. Eventually the couple were found by a search party sent out by a very angry father. The girl was brought back to the *bilek*, the marriage annulled, and the girl later made to marry the Iban lad

Young men dancing to break the monotony of fishing

originally chosen by her father. The author did not see this incident as a tragic thing in the young people's lives, for the Iban nature tends to accept that which it is difficult to change. Each eventually found happiness in the arranged marriage.

But this story is an unusual one. All Ibans love and spoil their children, and rare indeed is the parent who forces a child to do anything against its will. Formerly it was not uncommon for the government to be told that it need not build a school because the children did not want to attend. In this sense only, there is an extreme permissiveness.

Until about the age of twelve or fourteen the Iban child has nothing to do but play and possibly take on the task of occasionally looking after a baby brother or sister if it is a busy season for the adults in the ricefields. Sometime early in their teens girls start learning the field and household tasks from their mothers. They take a hand at guarding the rice plots during the crucial ripening season and help prepare food for the family who are at work all day planting or harvesting. At sixteen, girls are adult field hands.

The young boys, however, at twelve or fourteen enter a much more exciting training period. Iban men love adventure and excitement in their lives and habitually leave the monotonous work of the fields to the women. Until he is in his middle thirties or approaching forty, a man may never have worked in the ricefields other than on the task of clearing and burning the trees and underbrush. The young lad will learn many skills from his father or older brother: how to paddle and pole a canoe without capsizing it, how to net fish and hunt. Early

Making a mat from long strips of bark interwoven with rattan. This is men's work

Hats from natural and dyed rattan are made by women

Weaving tools such as this shuttle of tapang *wood are sometimes beautifully carved*

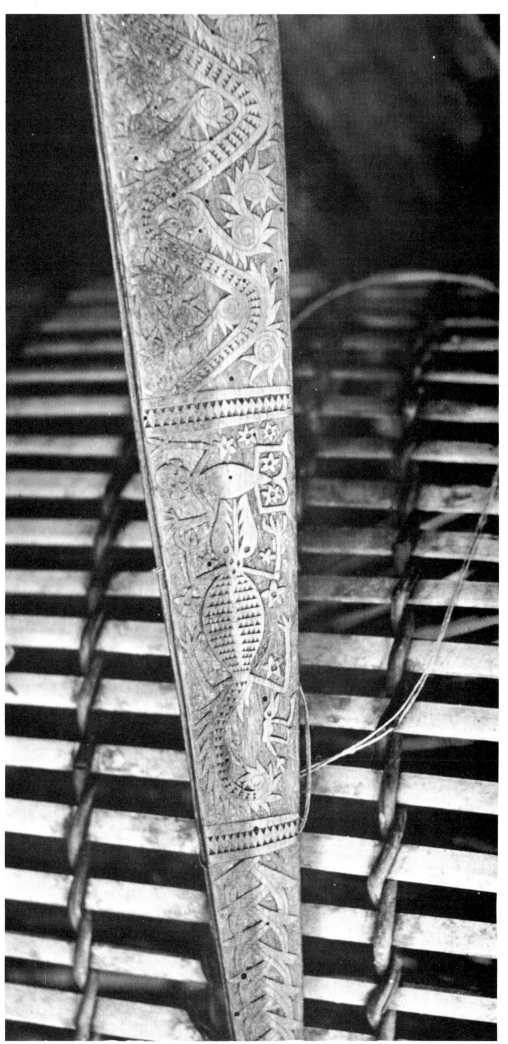

Another shuttle, carved with human, animal, and plant motifs

Women at the daily chore of husking rice on a longhouse veranda

A large fishtrap being made. The river fish are generally quite small

Women occasionally dress up as men and put on masks to dance on festive occasions

The Ibans locate their cemeteries in shady places by the riverside

Ibans dislike facial hair. They shave, rub their skin with stones, and pluck out individual hairs

Pouring rice beer with a coconut shell

There is great variety in Iban faces. Some girls look almost Chinese

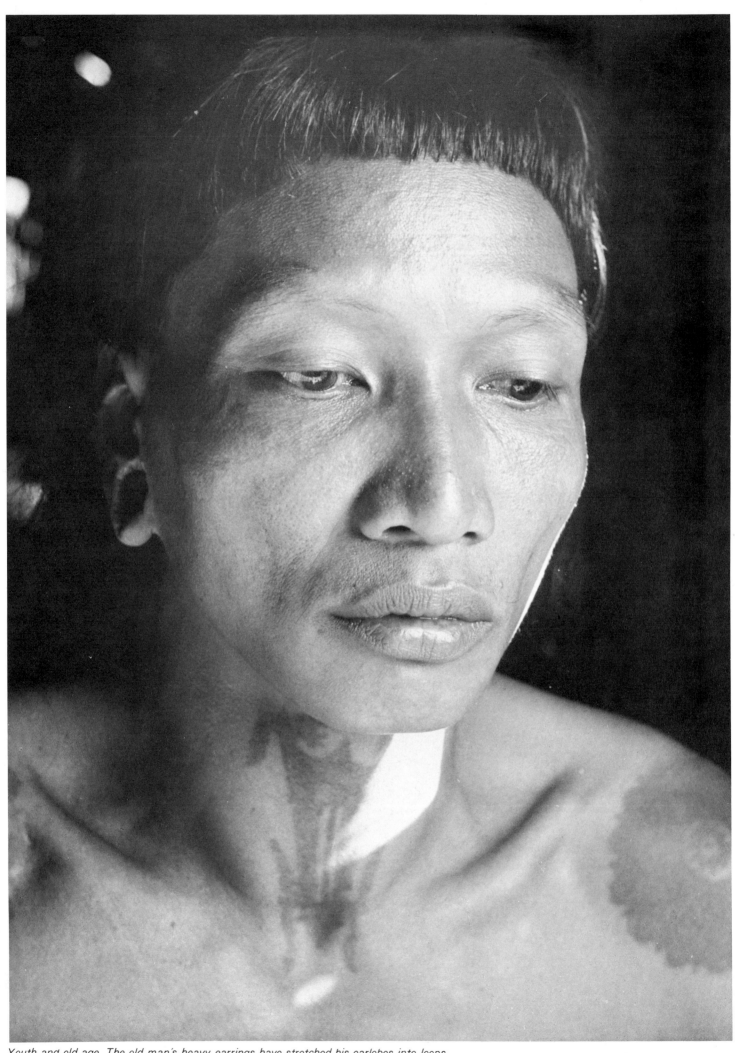

Youth and old age. The old man's heavy earrings have stretched his earlobes into loops

There is little sugar in the Iban diet. They delight in finding bees' nests

A tame baby hornbill being fed

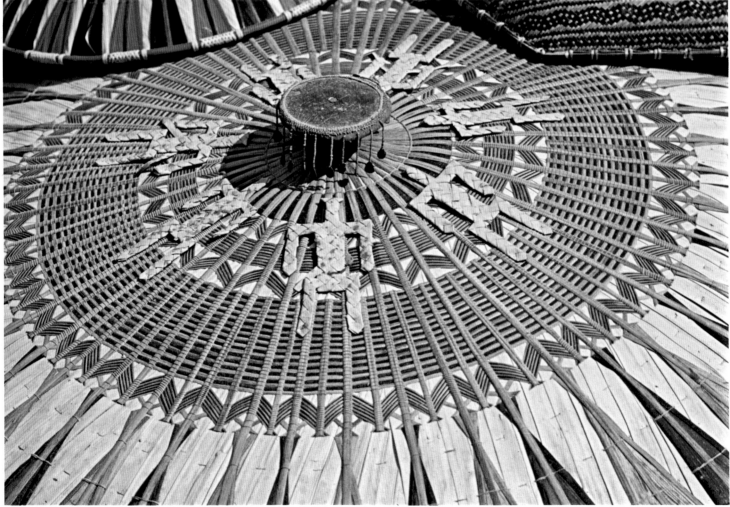

The variety of shapes and patterns of hats is endless

on, he will develop a strong desire to wander, to go on journeys to conduct some item of family business or simply to explore the countryside and the river and its tributaries. And he may well spend more time visiting girls in another longhouse than he spends in his family *bilek*.

Until such time as he is called upon to take over the responsibility for the family farm by the age or incapacity or death of his father, the Iban male lives a carefree and adventurous life. When he finally accepts the settled life of a farmer he may very well be a complete tyro—a stranger to the job of farming. In this art it is the Iban women who excel, and the males are usually required only to do the heaviest work.

Ibans are a gregarious lot and love a party. Any excuse will do, whether it is an important event such as a birth or a wedding, or merely the return of a longhouse member from a long journey, or the visit of a government official. The dancing usually begins early and goes on until dawn. The most impressive and popular dances are those that enact battle scenes of old. With full formal regalia of monkey cape, hornbill feathers, sword, and shield, the dancing warriors alternate with agility and superb control from a slow-motion swaying movement to a leap and thrust accompanied by a fierce shout, and then back again to a slow movement. In their turn, other men will come forward to show their particular skill in variations on the same choreographic theme, and the evening becomes a long competition, growing more and more noisy and uninhibited as the night passes.

If the entertainment is not to be a war-dance competition, some group will start a line in which others join until everyone is moving rhythmically in file up and down the longhouse gallery, swaying first to one side, then to the other. This may also go on till the early hours or until one by one the participants drop out of the line from sheer exhaustion.

At all these parties great quantities of *tuak*, or rice beer, are drunk. First of all the male guests are welcomed with a cup of the mild brew. The wise ones will merely touch the cup to the lips and pass it back to the girl who presented it. By custom she should then drain the cup, and sometimes she does. As the dances begin and the *tuak* flows, the noise of laughter and shouted conversation becomes deafening. The orchestra of small gongs and drums made of monkeyskin stretched across the end of a hollowed log add to the cacophony. To the untrained ear there will seem to be no order or measure to the sounds. But at some distance, on a peaceful jungle night, the gamelanlike music makes a pleasant sound as it comes across the warm dark air.

Iban women sometimes take a part in the battle dances with the men. Each warrior will partner one particular girl in his jumps and gyrations, while she moves with slow and measured rhythm. As the *tuak* flows and inhibitions relax, the dances frequently become mating dances, with the full gamut of suggestive movements and glances.

During the slack season in the fields—and it is during that season that the Ibans do their entertaining—those who stayed till the end of a party will sleep away half of the following day and perhaps resume the party the following night. On great occasions such as the traditional bird festivals, or *gawai burong*, the feasting and dancing may continue for several days and nights, stopping only for rest and to allow the women to prepare more food.

At these important entertainments no expense is spared on food and decor. All the headmen from up and down the river are invited. Hopefully a government official will grace the longhouse by his presence at the festival. All the most decorative and treasured woven mats are spread on the *ruai* or hung against the wall or over bamboo rods. The favorite dishes of rice cake, fish, pork, and vegetables are prepared in quantity.

According to strict tradition, the bird festival consists of nine separate festivals or stages. In the old days only a warrior who returned from battle with newly taken enemy heads could think of playing host at a bird festival. In later warfare, if he were again successful, he could give another party each time new heads were procured. Few warriors ever exhausted the nine stages of the *gawai burong* series, and those who did have become legendary heroes in the folk stories of the Ibans.

At the beginning of the bird festival party the spirits must be respectfully welcomed and provided for. A tray of *tuak* and small dishes containing samples of all the delicacies prepared is formally set out, blessed, and hung up in the rafters of the house to nourish the spirits. Only then may the feasting and entertainment begin. Toward the end of the festival a large stylized, carved and gaily painted wooden hornbill may be hoisted to the top of a pole. The *kenyalang*, or hornbill bird, is the sacred Dayak symbol of the bird god *Sengalang Burong*, who is the god of warfare and of valor.

Nowadays few occasions of war and none of headtaking can be found for the bird festival, so in recent years the festival has been held in several longhouses to honor the members of the Sarawak Rangers who fought successfully against the Communist guerrillas during the Malayan emergency and for other such reasons. Frequently a good rice harvest will be celebrated by a bird festival, and sometimes a prominent and popular Iban who has performed some significant service for his people plays host at a *gawai burong*.

The bird as a symbol in Dayak mysticism and its use as an augury on all important occasions is widespread among the Borneo pagans. But Ibans have developed to a high degree the legends and ritual that surround augury. The giant hornbill is the most sacred symbol, but a chicken or cockerel is most commonly used in ceremonies, perhaps because these fowl are plentiful. At weddings a chicken is held over the heads of the couple, just as it is used to bless people departing from the longhouse on some journey of importance. And an honored visitor is greeted on arrival at the longhouse by the sacrifice of a chicken, or sometimes a pig which is later roasted and eaten.

There are other symbolic animals. Warriors see the spirit of bravery and martial success in snakes—the most auspicious being the hamadryad or king cobra—so snakes are not needlessly killed, and it is a bad omen to look at their charred remains after the fields are burned over in August.

Omens are frequently read into bird calls and also into the particular flight path of a bird across the sky or at the horizon. It may sometimes seem odd, among such a practical and outgoing people as the Ibans, that the spirits occupy such a prominent place in life. But at least the Ibans are not the total slaves of their mystical ideas. Their universe, both in its practical and its animistic aspects, is reasonably well under their control.

THE RICE CYCLE

The day in a longhouse begins early, long before dawn while the heavy, humid dark of the Borneo skies still keeps the jungle in thrall, making it a mysterious and eery place. Before dawn, for a few short hours, there is comparative quiet in the jungle. Birds seem asleep, the insects are dormant, and the still air lets the leaves and creepers, the matted vegetable growth, hang quiet in the gloom. Only an occasional whisper as one growing leaf springs over another, and perhaps the small buzz of a nocturnal winged creature, break the silence; and occasionally, at the jungle's edge, is heard the sudden whirr of a bat swooping in search of its last prey before returning home.

The longhouse, never far from the skirts of the jungle, is also still. Everyone is asleep; even the pigs under the floor have ceased to rootle and grunt. So the sudden shriek of a fighting cock, restive as it senses the approach of day, echoes with shattering, almost alarming volume through the rafters and over the night air. Sometimes it would seem these fighting cocks—one to almost every family in the building— are incurable insomniacs, for at any hour of the night one of other of them lets out its cry like some despairing soul lost in the ghost-ridden dark. With the approach of dawn the cocks stir and start a dialogue of raucous challenge, as if eager to be at one another's throats.

They are the heralds of the new day. Their challenge is soon taken up—by dogs, by early cicadas with their faltering and insidious strumming and sawing that swells imperceptibly to the full-throated chorus of day. Early birds, too, send out their curious melodic or random calls, sounds that come clear over the cool predawn air. And the sky lightens to a somber gray. The dogs begin their morning round of sniffing and low growling under the house and around the clearing.

Then the human inhabitants begin to stir. The freshness of the dawn air in Borneo makes it no hardship to rise. The women are generally first, coming down the notched log that is the stairway from the longhouse in ones and twos on their way to the river to bathe. The sun is not yet over the heads of the dark trees, but its light now tinges the sky with dull orange—orange that turns, as you watch, to yellow, then to palest yellow, and is crowned by a deep blue zenith. The women and girls greet the day with splashing and chatter as they bathe in the river, often playing games in the shallows like their children.

By the time they are coming back to the longhouse, laden with long baskets slung on their backs, the sun has cleared the yellow from the sky and its rays luminesce on a cloud or two in the pale blue dome against which the trees have become sharp silhouettes. The baskets contain long segments of fat bamboos, the water containers of the jungle people. This is the first journey of the day for water, and many more have to be made during its course by the women and girls, and even old grandmothers, for the river is their only source. It is a rare longhouse, indeed, even today, that boasts a piped water supply.

By the time the womenfolk return, the men have got up, and many of them are on their way down to the riverbank to wash in their turn. While the wives build little fires in crude earthenware or clay fireplaces and the smoke begins to drift up blue above the longhouse roof, they too return, often settling down to smoke and gossip among themselves if it is the slack season in the fields. At planting or harvesting times, of course, the early morning is full of the bustle of preparation for a start on the day's work—tools and baskets, all the implements and impedimenta appropriate to the day's activities, being collected and set out in readiness for departure to the fields.

The breakfast rice is now boiling in iron caldrons or in Chinese cooking pots. With it the Ibans like to eat a morsel of salted fish or some vegetables left over from the previous evening's meal. Sometimes there is even a bit of pork. The Ibans have taken to the Chinese habit of tea-drinking. They prefer their tea laced with sugar and condensed milk—as indeed do many Chinese in Borneo and other places, a habit quite unlike the traditional Chinese savoring of the delicate bouquet of small steaming cups of tea innocent of milk or sugar. If there is a guest in the longhouse it is quite common for an Iban wife to serve what she considers an honorable substitute for tea—instant coffee in a mug or boiled in one of her collection of useful cans kept for various purposes. With the addition of condensed milk and the gray-colored sugar of local origin, the beverage is a murky color and not very inviting to the taste.

Breakfast over, the morning's work begins for everyone except the small children, the dogs, the pigs now grunting beneath the floorboards, and the petted fighting cocks that have already been fondled by the men, just as they fondle their babies, and with equal pride.

Rice is the life-sustaining crop of the Ibans, as it is of all Borneo and Southeast Asia. In the growing season, the long months between planting and harvesting, the women are off to the fields of hill paddy soon after breakfast while the morning is still young and cool, to continue where they left off the day before the backbreaking and never-ending task of weeding among the rice plants. The men make their morning rounds among the rubber trees, collecting the milky latex in earthen pots and cutting diagonal slashes in the bark of the trees to encourage fresh latex to flow. The collected latex is poured into shallow pans and treated with hydrochloric acid. Coagulated sheets of raw rubber are then smoked and draped over bamboo rods to dry. Every few days the rubber sheets are packed onto long *perahu*s and transported downriver to the nearest Chinese shop or trading post or cooperative store where they are sold for cash or bartered for supplies. Along with his rubber, the Iban may take to market small lots of jungle fruit such as coconuts, pineapples, durians, and mangosteens, as well as yams and gourds and beans from his garden patch. The salable crops of rubber, fruit, and vegetables provide the Ibans with their only steady and reliable source of cash.

Until recent years the Ibans had no need of money and little knowledge of it. Personal debts were paid in kind, usually rice, and the door or *bilek* tax which every household owed to the government in Kuching, amounting to f1 per annum, could also be paid in grain at the rate of one *pasu*, or about a bushel. Payment of large debts and fines, and other exchanges of relatively big amounts of wealth, was facilitated by the exchange of the Chinese porcelain jars so valued by all Dayaks or of old brass cannon and gongs, almost equal to the jars in value to their owners. As one observer has pointed out, there must be a fortune in Chinese Ming, K'ang-hsi, and Ch'ien-lung porcelain in some Iban longhouses, whether or not the owners know its true value. The occasional Sung and T'ang pieces of pottery are highly prized by Ibans, but ceramic pots from the early Chinese contacts are now most usually found by the Sarawak Museum's excavations in shards, many of them painstakingly pieced together for study and display in Kuching. Doweries and bride price and other large transactions were made by a rough scale of values attached to the jars. For example, the most

Reaping the paddy harvest

An old woman and a man in a temporary shelter near the ricefields

Burning the jungle in preparation for planting rice

valuable, the *menaga* jar, was said to be worth one human life. In exchange value it equaled two of the less valuable *rusa* jars. The *rusa*, in turn, was the equivalent of two *alas* jars, each of which had the value of two *panding* jars. The least valuable jar, the *irun*, was worth two or three China plates.

The valuable jars were not only the medium of important business transactions; but a rough code of practical justice within Iban *adat*, or commonly accepted law, centered on them. A blood feud between families or between villages could be settled by the payment of a prescribed value in jars. In such an exchange, an *alas* jar was paid to an injured party for a physical insult suffered at the hands of a neighbor or an enemy from another village. For the accidental or even premeditated killing of an Iban, his family could expect a *menaga* jar at

the least. And the fine, according to an old and honored tradition, *pati nyawa*, could amount to two old and valuable jars. Failing this, the killer would be expected to surrender himself to the victim's family, he and his children to be their slaves.

Some old jars are said to possess oracular value, divined by the sound made when water is poured into them, and this, doubtless, is merely an extension of the value normally placed on them.

Second only to the Chinese jars, brass gongs and small cannon, usually of Brunei origin, were the medium of exchange in large deals. One famous longhouse chief demanded and received for the hand of his beautiful daughter the following bride price or *drian*: one large carrying basket of fresh enemy heads, a brass cannon, a hundred chickens, a sow, and a brass gong called *sanda kaki*, the gong to be

The hillside still smoking after the fire

used as the bride's footrest during the wedding ceremony.

In recent years money economy has crept up the rivers of Sarawak, and now all but the most traditional ceremonial exchanges are made in coins and paper money. In dealings with a Chinese shopkeeper the Ibans invariably come off second best. Wallace long ago felt strongly that the simple, honest Iban was the prey of the Chinese and Malay who "cheat and plunder them continually." The Chinese have known money from ancient times and they have a healthy respect for the earning power of a dollar. The commercial Chinese does not hoard his dollars but invests them in one way or the other—an almost religious operation to the Chinese. Consequently Chinese have no use for the savings cooperatives that have sprung up in the Iban longhouses. Unlike the Chinese, the Iban has only recently discovered the 'magic paper,' and

paper money is a commodity which easily slips through his hands and not infrequently finds its way back to the Chinese shopkeeper in exchange for some object of necessity or, not infrequently, something that merely takes his fancy. The Ibans have tried savings cooperatives in efforts to build up capital in the longhouse, but success has been variable. In many cases Ibans have been able to save and invest capital cooperatively to bring modern innovations to the village. Such conveniences as electricity (usually from a diesel generator), rice mills, motor launches, and more sturdy and finished building materials for the longhouse are not uncommon in Iban villages. Yet the greatest deterrent to modernism is still the conservatism and the tradition-bound nature of the Dayaks themselves. And perhaps not so much their conservatism as their lackadaisical and easygoing approach to life. The Ibans en

Holes are made in the ground with poles, and the grains dropped into them.

masse may show great initial enthusiasm for a new project, but to move them from their *tuak* and gossip to accomplishment is another thing altogether. Each one may well decide that it is the other fellow's job. As one observer expressed it, "There is a tremendous gap between their determination to do things and their actual performance."

In the present century another way by which the Ibans supplement their income has developed. The young Iban man, always fond of wandering, has been recruited for work on the rubber plantations and oil fields along the coast and in Brunei. Some have contracted out to work as far afield as Malaya in such jobs as are offered by the public works and land survey in Johore. The extra income brought back to the longhouse has increased the prosperity of the *bilek* family and re-

duced its dependence upon rice. To some extent, therefore, the vagaries of the rice yield have had a less drastic affect upon the fortunes of the family than formerly. In modern jargon, the Iban has learned a rudimentary diversification of occupation. The modern meaning however can be deceiving in the case of Ibans, for the young warrior would rather go to work in a distant place, thus returning with the great prestige so necessary for Iban self-respect, than accept casual employment locally. Iban unemployment, especially during depressions or declines in the world rubber market, has been an extremely complicated social problem in twentieth-century Sarawak. Indeed the young Iban man will very reluctantly settle down to a rice-growing and farming responsibility, and then only when the older men of the *bilek* are no

Weeding a ricefield. In the foreground is the roof of a shelter from which a guard can watch the crop

longer able to shoulder these agricultural burdens.

But while rubber trees, fruit crops, and work in the oil fields and on downriver farms supplement the income from growing rice, it is still the rice harvest which represents prosperity to the Iban longhouse dwellers. If the rice stalks are heavy and the crop is good it will be a bountiful and happy year. If not, the Iban will attempt with varying degrees of success to make up the loss by selling his rubber and fruit. Usually it is a futile attempt, for his fruit and vegetables are not the best, having been grown rather haphazardly in untidy, neglected, and unsuitable plots in corners and crannies of land. Iban rubber is of poor quality because of impurities and invariably fetches the lowest prices from the Chinese dealers, who even at the best of times buy as cheaply as possible.

Rice, then, is the staff of life in Iban country, and it is no exaggeration to say that the whole rhythm of life in the longhouse, year in and year out, revolves about the rice crop. Nor is rice merely an economic factor. To a very large degree rice growing is the religion of the long house, and rice grain is the subject of animist worship by Ibans. The agricultural cycle is governed by a complicated system of beliefs and surrounded by periodic and established ceremonial. Ritual at planting time, ritual at the harvest, and ceremonies to protect the rice plant from the scourges of disease and pests and bad weather are given considerable attention by the longhouse inhabitants over the period from midsummer to late winter. An elaborate system of taboos, or *pemali,*

Carrying a load of harvested rice to the longhouse.

surrounds the agricultural process. This is hardly surprising, since at times during the growing season life in a longhouse is precarious indeed.

From the oldest times the Ibans, in common with many other Dayak communities, have practiced a type of rice culture which is both drudgery to the laborer and destructive and wasteful of the land. This is the slash and burn, plant and harvest cycle required of shifting hill rice agriculture.

Each *bilek* family has its assigned plot of land and grows its own crop separately from its neighbors. Yet, as a village, the whole agricultural cycle is accomplished in concert and harmony—from the first selection of the land to be worked, the clearing, the planting, the tending, and the harvesting—by a cooperative effort and a rather com-

plicated yet practical system of work exchange. This exchange is based on a unit of half a day's work. The Iban may work a number of half days for his neighbor, thus building up a credit of half days which the neighbor must pay back later on. The *bilek*s of other longhouses are often involved in this half-day credit and debt system, and in the short and busy few weeks of harvest the transactions can become extremely complex. A strict reciprocity is adhered to. All half days must be worked off during the harvesting and all half-day debts on both sides thereby paid up. Historically, the seminomadic life of the Iban was dictated by the periodic need to find new farmland. Nowadays virgin jungle is rare, and plots of hill land are cultivated for two to five years and then left fallow. During the following fifteen to twenty years the ground reverts to jungle, and after that the farmers may return to plant it again. Thus the Iban

Waiting for a boat to cross a stream

farmer has usually to contend with the problems of clearing secondary or tertiary growth. Because of the movement to new plots every few years, the land close to the longhouse, which was cultivated first, is quickly used up, and each year the villagers' farms are farther away from the village, sometimes up to half a dozen miles away. The inconvenience of traveling by canoe, or on foot over difficult hill trails, between longhouse and farm adds to the problems facing the Iban rice farmer in his primitive agricultural life.

As travel from village to field becomes too long, a group of Ibans in a longhouse who are farming the same terrain get together and build a *dampa* or farmhouse, a second home, on the farm. In every detail the *dampa* resembles the longhouse except that it is smaller. Two to ten *bilek*s is the usual size, and perhaps less care is taken in construc-

tion since it is to be a temporary home. This becomes the family's home during the growing season from about August to late March. In this season some longhouses are almost entirely deserted. The *bilek* doors are locked, and a general air of abandonment surrounds the village. The longhouse comes to life again from April to July during the off season, and occasionally during the growing season if important visitors from outside or government district officers pay calls. At these times the families troop back over the jungle paths to the longhouse to prepare for and entertain the guests. But as soon as the visitors are out of sight, the migration back to the farmhouse begins.

When the fields under cultivation are close to the longhouse there is no need for a *dampa*. A small hut in the middle of the paddy is comfortable enough for the night watchers who guard the crop during

A rice storage bin in the loft of a longhouse

the most crucial times of the growing season.

The beginning of the rice season is governed by the position of the stars. When the cluster of Pleiades is observed at dawn in a particular location above the horizon during May, it is a signal to begin the selection of the land to be cultivated. The *tuai rumah* confers with *bilek* heads on the location and size of the farms, and the details of the initial rituals are agreed on.

Among the rituals performed is the whetstone ceremony. Most longhouse families have a sacred whetstone, often a small boulder dredged from a stream in the distant past and probably at that time used as an altar for the sacrifice of enemies taken in battle. The stone is nowadays the center of a rite in which food is consecrated, a chicken is killed and its blood spilled, and the proper spirits are invoked to help in the

coming season and to secure a bountiful crop.

At this time the farmland is just an area of tangled vines and scrub among which jungle giants stand above lesser trees. It is these giants—fifteen to twenty feet in girth—that constitute the challenge to the young men of the village. To fell one so that it falls in the most convenient place requires brawn, but also considerable skill. The clearing of jungle—especially of virgin jungle—is associated in some ways with the right of ownership. Most land, however, is covered by secondary jungle these days, having been cleared long ago and allowed to lie fallow for a decade or two. Nonetheless, it may well contain trees of a size that makes them no mean challenge for the youths of the longhouse.

On the appointed day of the *manggol* rites in May or early June

Threshing rice by trampling the ears underfoot

the head of each *bilek* family goes to his farm with offerings of cooked rice. There, in the middle of his plot, he will clear a few square feet and put up a rough hut or shelf on which to place the offerings to the land god, underneath which he will bury a root or piece of wood chosen at random, at the same time reciting a prayer to the god *Pulang Gana* asking for a good crop of rice. The ritual of *manggol* is surrounded by taboos and omens. No one may go to the fields for one full day following the rites. Certain animals, if observed, are omens of ill luck, and people plug their ears during the rite so as not to hear unfavorable omens—the bark of a deer or the cry of an omen bird. The whole period of *manggol* may last up to a month, from the selection of the farmland to the clearing of the undergrowth.

In June and July all the able-bodied members of the family set to with knives and small axes to clear the bushes and small trees. The task of felling the large trees is by tradition the privilege of the men. This is the one part of shifting rice cultivation to which the young Iban warriors take with alacrity. Felling the giants is a hazardous job requiring skill, courage, and not a little nimbleness, presenting an opportunity for a young man to display his prowess in competition with the other men of the village. The job has its own folklore—stories of the great woodsmen of the past pitted against the ancient virgin forests of the pioneering period. With headhunting and warfare no longer allowed by an ever-watchful government, the young Iban has little opportunity nowadays of prestige-building, and the felling of big trees, together with wandering to foreign parts, are welcome opportunities.

A frame platform is built against the tree to be cut, and from that

Newly planted pepper vines and the hardwood posts on which they will be trained

position two Ibans hack away at the trunk with large axes, nowadays usually of European type bought from Chinese or Malay traders. Formerly the Ibans made their own axes from metal imported, along with ceramics, from China and Siam (although it is thought by some that the ancestors of Ibans knew how to work iron long before they arrived in Borneo). As the tree falls the woodsmen quickly scramble from their platform to avoid being crushed by the trunk. To fell a tree in exactly the prescribed position is a difficult art, and this forms part of the challenge and adventure of the work. It is important for the trees to be neatly felled in line or against one another, as this facilitates burning, the next stage in the long work of preparing the jungle ground for the rice seed.

With the end of the clearing comes a worrisome time for the whole Iban community. A good stretch of dry weather with clear skies is es-

sential to dry out the piled-up branches and undergrowth before they can be fired and the earth exposed for planting. A wet August is useless, for then the clearing cannot be burned. Even though a few weeks of dry weather may still come in September, when firing and planting may finally take place, the season will by then usually be too far advanced, and planting will be late. Late-planted rice, according to ancient tradition, will not produce a plentiful crop. To ensure even a fair harvest, great attention must be paid to the gods. Offerings and rites are constant activities in the growing season, and omens good and bad must be heeded. Meteorological conditions during late summer can doom the whole Iban community to hunger and hardship for the coming year or bless it with abundance.

When the undergrowth is set on fire, the farmers shout incanta-

Tapping a rubber tree. Rubber is the Ibans' main cash crop

tions to the spirits in the wind to blow a strong blast and make a good blaze. In a good season everything will be tinder-dry and the flames will consume even the largest felled trees, only logs left unburned being dragged to one side to be burned separately later on. The whole area becomes a sad-looking, black, charred landscape. The Ibans know the ash is good for the crop, but the burning is not done primarily to make fertilizer but simply to clear the dense growth.

For a day afterward, a taboo restricts everyone from the burned fields. In this way people will avoid seeing any dead animals caught in the fire, for to see them is a bad omen and in some instances a prediction of death in the *bilek* during the rice season. A day or so later the sowing takes place, usually as a communal activity involving several families or even the whole village. Men drill the holes and women drop

in the rice seeds. When all the farms have been planted, each *bilek* family tends its own plots.

As planting begins several plates of offerings are once more presented to the earth god at a small altar. Then the husband and wife on whose ground the day's planting is to take place begin sowing, followed by all the other adults involved. The men move across the plots with pointed wooden staffs five or six feet long, driving three-inch holes in the earth with a quick thrust and twist of the hand. As the farm is usually on hilly terrain and some logs and stumps are left from the burning, this method makes it possible to reach into nooks and corners and prepare the whole plot for the seed.

The women's job is more arduous. Carrying the seed in a metal cup or small rattan basket in the left hand, each woman drops several

Pepper vines growing in orderly rows

Sheets of coagulated rubber being washed prior to smoking

kernels into each hole. Moving after the men, they must scramble over and around charred logs and stumps, locating the holes and planting the seed with a deft and sure hand.

The Ibans use several varieties of rice, and the women are responsible for selecting the seed and the planting place for each variety. Working methodically over the whole area, each variety is sown according to its maturation period until, near the center of the fields and near the altar and ritual place, the sacred *padi pun* is planted with great care and reverence, surrounded by various 'magical' plants. Each Iban *bilek* family has its own highly regarded sacred rice seed, *padi pun*. In it reside the chief rice spirits, while lesser spirits are attached to the other varieties. All of the *padi pun* is never planted, thus ensuring that, should disaster overtake the farm and destroy the rice crop, some

of the sacred seed will remain for the next year's planting. But when, at harvesttime, the new *padi pun* is reaped, the old is ceremoniously eaten by the *bilek* family. Later on, reaping takes place in the same order as the planting, and the spirits of the rice which are released as the panicles are cut from the stock follow the women reapers in an unbroken path until at last the sacred rice is harvested and, along with the grain, the rice spirits are led back to the longhouse to be stored until another season. Extreme care must be taken not to lose the rice spirits in the period between their release in reaping and their arrival at the longhouse.

At the edge of the field, and sometimes between the rice plants, maize is planted, its shorter growing season allowing it to be harvested before the rice matures. Cucumbers, squash, pumpkin, and other vine

An Iban selling his rubber at a village shop

vegetables may be planted around stumps of trees and in small plots close to the longhouse. The government constantly encourages the planting of sago palms and pepper gardens as well. Sago is easy to grow and furnishes a staple starch food (though it is less palatable than rice) should the rice crop fail. Pepper, on the other hand, is a cash crop. But despite efforts to diversify crops, the Ibans still prefer to put most agricultural energy into hill rice, for rice is a part of religion as well as most of their livelihood.

Now begins the nurturing and guarding of the ricefields. Soon after the burning, a small watch hut is built in the midst of the fields, and when planting is complete some of the unburned logs are used to build a fence around the area to keep out the larger destructive animals such as wild pig and deer. A whole gamut of devices is employed to guard the crop. Traps are devised, and nowadays shotguns are ready at hand to rid the rice patch of large predators. A border or cleared strip around the field will sometimes be made in the belief that animals will hesitate to expose themselves on open ground. Poles are erected at intervals, noisemakers of dried bamboo attached to them. Lines stretched across the fields and connected at a central place in the watch hut have clattering objects and bits of bright cloth attached, so that when the watcher tugs on the line the whole network is set in motion to scare off birds and small animals. Gongs, too, may be used, and in the most crucial weeks of the maturing season the farmers patrol their ricefields night and day.

But against insect pests or diseases of the rice, the Ibans have only ritual to rely on. They call upon the good spirits to exorcise the evil

When the harvest is gathered, the season of festivals begins. The veranda of a longhouse is gaily decorated for that purpose

Model airplanes join the traditional hornbill carvings in the decorations for the festival

and rid them of the malign visitation. Should disease attack the rice the Ibans ceremoniously dig up a clump of the grain and transport it with loving care to the longhouse. There it is placed in a sacred spot and a member of the family attends the sick rice, calling upon the spirits to bring it back to health. Next day the cured rice is returned to the farm and replanted.

One way and another, the majority of Iban men manage to escape the most backbreaking work of the rice season—the weeding of the fields that starts almost as soon as planting is over and continues for about five months. This is considered women's work, although the old men sometimes lend a hand. The able-bodied male shuns the task in favor of pottering among his rubber and fruit trees, or better still going on an expedition. During the weeding season the young men

usually find an excuse for a journey, for weeding is monotonous, un-glamorous work and involves no ritual. If the man of the family must help with the weeding he does so only when other workers are away and when no women from outside the family are working on the farm. And even then he weeds as if in secret, for it is unseemly for his neighbors, especially the neighbor women, to see him at such undignified women's work. The custom is changing, however, and as more and more women are relieved of the field work men are appearing in the women's traditional role in the fields. When women assume their primary role as housemakers, it is usually a sign of prosperity in the family. And Iban men prefer the prestige and luxury of having their women attend to their comfort at home whenever possible. This is possible when they can afford to hire help in the fields from less prosperous

Model airplanes are raised high on tall poles near the longhouse

members of the longhouse.

By March the crop has begun to ripen and the harvest rituals begin. Before reaping starts it must be properly inaugurated by tying a clump of stalks with red thread and placing an offering under them. Then some of the earliest ripened grain is taken to the longhouse and a thanksgiving meal is eaten in the evening. Even the wandering young men will return to the longhouse for this important new-rice ritual.

Reaping is done mostly by the women. Using short knives which fit the hand, and with baskets slung in front of them, they move through the rice, cutting first the well ripened panicles. Larger and deeper baskets are used by men to transport the paddy to the longhouse. When loaded, some of these carrying baskets weigh as much as 100 pounds, and the transporting of such heavy loads over the rough jungle

paths to the longhouse is a feat of strength and stamina much admired among the Iban men. Next to felling the forest this is the part of the rice growing season where the man of the family excels. The arrival of the first baskets of paddy in the village is greeted by an elaborate rite to welcome them into the longhouse. A woman meets the first basket of rice and offers the bearer some *tuak*, and some of the beer is poured ceremoniously before the rice is emptied into large rattan mats. Then offerings are made and the rice panicles are bundled into the mat for temporary storage.

Threshing is quick work compared to reaping. The panicles are spread on open mats in the longhouse gallery and trodden by both men and women. It is happy although strenuous work, and rhythmic treading becomes a sort of lighthearted ritual dance. Winnowing is done on the

Dressing for a festival after bathing in the river

Longhouse men in ceremonial costume with rifles and swords decorated with hornbill feathers

longhouse veranda, the broken rice and partly filled husks being set aside, sometimes to be sold to the local Chinese shopkeeper, sometimes to be ground and eaten first before the whole grain is used.

After being spread and dried in the hot tropical sun for several days the rice is gathered and stored in large bins in the loft of the *bilek;* and storage, too, is a ritual activity, for the spirits of the rice have to be properly guided and escorted to their resting place in the bins. Rice must not be carelessly stepped on or spilled through cracks in the floor of the longhouse, for if the rice spirits are offended they may depart and leave the family with poor harvests for some years to come.

For the Ibans, everything connected with the rice cycle is ascribed to the well-being or unhappiness of the indwelling rice spirits. Attention is given to ritual rather than to agronomy. The precarious nature of primitive jungle agriculture and the fact that the Iban farmer at the best of times stands close to the threshold of agricultural ruin has given rise to the mystical atmosphere that surrounds every step in rice growing. In a very real sense, rice growing itself is at the heart of Iban religion and Iban life.

During the growing season the workday for the field hands begins soon after dawn and continues to late afternoon. Midday brings food and a short rest in the forest shade at the edge of the fields. Some women will remain in the fields working in the cool hours at the end of the day to catch up with the weeding, and when the rice is maturing the family guard the plots night and day.

The Ibans' leisure time is not during the rice season, except for the occasional visit of a government official who must be properly entertained with *tuak* and dancing. But when the harvest is in and safely stored, and when each *bilek* has either bemoaned the bad harvest or rejoiced at its prosperity—then comes the time for making merry. At this time any casual visitor is the excuse for a party. The women, relaxing after months of toil in the fields, dress up in their most colorful sarongs, and the young men in their hornbill feathers and monkey-fur vests prepare for the dance competition while others tune the crude stringed instrument called *sapek*, and gongs and drums start to sound.

The visitor is the honored guest at the party but also, unknown to him, the victim of a conspiracy to get him as drunk as possible on rice beer. The man who can down a whole cup of *tuak* in one draft is applauded—and well might he be, for *tuak* is on the raw side to non-Dayak taste. But, admirable as the act may be, it is unwise; for the drinking goes on all night and the hero may be expected to repeat the performance endlessly. He will also be expected to perform a dance and will be urged on by the young girls of the house.

At this leisurely spring season when the rice has been harvested, the wanderlust of the Iban men revives. Out of the long lazy hours in the *bilek* or lounging in the *ruai*, and from the gossip and chatter of this free time, come ideas for journeys to friends and relatives in distant parts, ideas for parties or for an expedition to the town to see what can be had in the bigger Chinese shops, or plans to hold a hornbill festival.

There is just enough work to be done in the vegetable and fruit plots and in tending the rubber trees to keep everyone out of mischief, but not enough to discourage speculation on everything under the Iban sun. It is a time for refreshing the tired body, a much awaited pause in the tyranny of the rice cycle, and comes as near to being a mass annual holiday as does the month of August for the average Parisian.

The off-season is also the time for weaving intricately patterned rattan mats for the *bilek* and for making the beautiful patterned blankets that are used as covers and for ornamenting the walls at festival times.

Spring is also the time for weddings. An Iban marriage is a fairly simple ceremony prefaced by long and elaborate preliminaries. There is much coming and going between the parents of the couple, since a thousand details have to be mutually agreed and arranged—all of which takes more time than one might imagine. But when everything is settled and the appointed day comes, the bride has to be brought from her longhouse to that of the groom, and this is done with due ceremony. A procession of the young man's relatives and friends, all in their best festive regalia, sets out and makes its way through the fields accompanied by a tremendous noise of clashing gongs and pounding of drums. The noise is directed as much toward preventing anyone's hearing inauspicious and ominous sounds as it is toward celebrating the occasion. When the bride is brought to the groom's longhouse the actual ceremony is brief. The couple are seated on big brass gongs and an elder waves a cockerel over their heads in a form of blessing and consecration. The newlyweds are required to live for three successive days and nights in the husband's longhouse, followed by three in that of the bride. After that, the marriage is accepted as properly complete. There is, of course, one escape route still open to the couple should they not find their marriage propitious. If either one or the other has a bad dream or hears some inauspicious sound during those six days and nights, the marriage can be annulled.

The ceremonies connected with death in the Iban milieu are even more elaborate and strange. The body lies in state on the floor of the *ruai*, surrounded by many fine woven hangings. Token possessions of the deceased are prepared to accompany him on his journey to the grave and onward to *Sabayon*—the next world in which Ibans believe most fervently. The corpse is buried amid much waving of chickens, scattering of rice, and sprinkling of fresh chicken blood. Elaborate precautions have to be taken to prevent the spirit of the deceased from returning to the longhouse from the cemetery with the mourners, and the last person to leave the grave beats a pole on the earth to scare away the ghost and obviate any likelihood of its following. Three days' mourning is observed, but this is by no means the end of the rites. Once every fifteen or twenty years a great *gawai antu*, or feast of the departed ones, is held in the longhouse to honor and remember all who have died since the last festival of this type. Complex rituals are gone through at this time, to the accompaniment of sacrifices of chickens and much eating and drinking. Ceremonial wine is drunk by selected warriors, and the many stages of the ritual are brought to a close with the erection of large and elaborately carved monuments at the graves.

With these and many another lesser festival and rite, each coming according to the season, the longhouse year continues, following ancient customs long hallowed and often eagerly awaited by the inhabitants. And come May and June, the familiar and in many ways comfortable and expectable cycle of life begins again with the first discussions on the new year's rice cycle around which virtually the whole of Iban life traditionally revolves.

A young man in traditional bracelets, earrings, and beads plays the sape

Girls wearing elaborate silver headdresses

Dancing becomes more and more lively as the night goes on

Children learning to dance at a longhouse celebration

A feast for men who returned from soldiering in Malaya in the 1950s

Women arriving at a longhouse for a party

Girls singing a song of welcome to a guest in the longhouse

Gaily painted hornbill carvings ready to be hoisted onto poles

Figures of Westerners stand on the tail of a huge hornbill carving

Formerly sounded in time of danger, gongs now summon people to festive occasions

The drums are made of wood and deerskin

The warrior dance with shield and sword is popular with the longhouse people

Hornbill feathers, goatskin cape, silver bracelets, and tassels of goat hair form the costume of the dancer.

Young men and girls during an informal evening

Women seldom dance but often play brass gongs. The silver dollars are Dutch

A musical instrument called engkruri, *possibly Chinese in origin*

THE IMPACT OF THE MODERN WORLD

In Sarawak, more than in any other region of Borneo, an attempt was made over a period of a hundred years by the authorities in whose hands the destinies of the peoples lay to cushion the impact of commercial imperialism on the Dayaks and Malays. The authorities during that time were the rajahs of the Brooke dynasty, whose policies of paternalism and protection were carried out by means of restricting the activities of European merchants and companies to simple trade and barter relations with the people. No great commercial plantation developments were allowed in Sarawak. It was thus only slowly that Western ways and world economics crept up the rivers of Sarawak and began changing traditional thought and challenging the pagan tribalism of the Ibans. The modern world has impinged on Iban longhouse society increasingly since the end of World War II. And yet old ways, old patterns of livelihood persist, and the rhythm of life still revolves around the longhouse and the growing of rice; and the tribal myths linger to a remarkable degree.

Nonetheless, the effect of modern government and economics upon traditional longhouse life has been marked. At the time when the second rajah's style of ruling was passing, under the lead of departmental heads in the third rajah's administration the government began tightening up and extending the actual authority of Kuching. Regulations and rumors of regulations proliferated, bewildering the longhouse people at a time when the residents were not sufficiently in touch with them to explain the government's purpose and to allay their fears.

In an attempt to regulate the collection of taxes, the door tax was extended to all *bilek*s including those occupied by the elderly and the very poor, who had traditionally been exempted. Ibans had never objected to the door tax, a tradition stretching back to the days of the Brunei authority, but they were angered by the injustice of taxing the less fortunate members of the longhouse. They also deeply resented a tax on firearms at a time in the early 1920's when the shotgun was coming into use against animals that destroyed the paddy. Rumors of other taxes were rife, some of them absurd. Some Ibans believed the government was going to impose a fifty-cent tax upon a man whenever he slept with his wife. Stories like these fostered a sense of grievance which was all the more keen for the lack of the old style of personal contact with the rajah's representatives.

Added to these discontents, Kuching's attempt to control Iban migration and wandering restricted the Ibans' sense of freedom, if not their actual freedom. For two reasons the government in the 1930's felt compelled to restrict the Ibans' movement. First, in order to administer government better and more efficiently, it was thought necessary to stabilize longhouse communities. Second, for soil conservation purposes restrictions had to be placed upon the destructive, shifting hill paddy culture. Fixed points beyond which Ibans could not slash and burn were established. Some areas of jungle were closed entirely to native activity, and even the collection of wild jungle fruit was prohibited in these forest reserves. Later the restricted reserves gave way to protected forests in which habitation was prohibited but in which Iban activity of a nondestructive type was allowed.

Uncontrolled shifting cultivation depletes the land and leaves it barren after continued cultivation for a number of years. Nature, however, has a way of restoring fertility if sufficient fallow time is allowed.

Before World War II, the government began to settle the Ibans and encourage crop diversification. No longhouse, it said, should contain fewer than ten *bilek*s, and young Iban males must have passes for traveling from district to district. Government's good intentions resulted in a severe curtailment of the Iban's time-honored habit of moving about in search of virgin farmland and going on expeditions, *bejalai*, for adventure and additional cash income.

In recent years these restrictions have been eased for the one-third of the population engaged in hill paddy farming, since it is now recognized that for a long time to come slash and burn culture will remain the chief occupation of the Ibans.

Encouraging the Ibans to grow other crops such as rubber also had its problems. Rubber is a very sensitive commodity on the modern world's capitalist market, as Malaya has found to its discomfiture in recent years. Small rubber holdings expose the Ibans to the whims of the world market price, and in times of depression or during periods of falling prices, dependence upon rubber planting can be disastrous. As early as 1929, repercussions of the world depression in agriculture were beginning to be felt along the rivers of Sarawak. The prices of rubber and jungle produce were declining, and Ibans who had for some time been venturing forth to the coastal areas and to Sabah and Malaya, to return with hard cash earnings from working these products, were hard hit. Likewise those longhouses which had diversified into the growing of rubber trees now found the profits greatly reduced. It was, of course, the Chinese and Malay rubber farmers of the lower rivers who were the real sufferers. But the depression hit the whole state, in common with other areas of Southeast Asia. Naturally enough, Ibans of the interior were less able to understand what was happening and were quick to blame the remote bureaucrats of Kuching.

The government's attempts to alter Iban slash and burn farming ran up against stubborn adherence to the traditions of the rice spirits and proved only marginally beneficial. The third rajah's government was bound sooner or later to run foul of the complexities of *adat*, or customary law, in its desire to regulate and standardize. Officials respected native *adat* and only slowly introduced English legal forms, but each Iban community tended to have its own version of *adat*, so the job of the magistrate was extremely difficult. Government was blamed more and more for wrong interpretation of *adat* in court cases. Yet obviously Kuching had to face the problem if its authority was to reach the farthest corners of the state.

Under the third rajah's regime the Ibans' inclination to resist authority and to rebel increased. In the late 1920's the tendency to resort to arms against a distant ruler's 'unjust' regulations and overpent-up grievances was very much alive. War spears were sent around to the longhouses in some areas of the Rajang River to call out the warriors to do battle. Asun's rebellion, named after its Iban leader, may have been the last remnant of earlier and wilder days of piracy and head-taking, and the Brookes treated it as such by mounting punitive expeditions, systematically burning longhouses, destroying the crops, and arresting offending Ibans. Not a few heads were taken, along the way, by the loyal Iban members of the Sarawak constabulary.

It is certain that the warrior ethos remained strong among the more remote Ibans, but to call the rebellion a 'recrudescence of headhunting' was probably wrong. During the days of the occupation of

A new school at Melugu, five hours' walk south of Simanggang on the Lupar River

Borneo in World War II, the Japanese troops did indeed face a real recrudescence of head-taking. They had more to fear from the Iban head-seekers in occupied Sarawak than from any allied military threat. Almost every longhouse claimed a few Japanese heads; and the inhabitants of one Iban longhouse each day carefully polished the spectacles still attached to one such gruesome trophy, said to have been the head of a Japanese colonel. Hence the occupation forces remained mainly in the towns in the lower rivers and left the interior tribes to themselves.

Seeking to bridge the gap between modernized natives and Europeans and the 'truly rural' natives, in the early 1930's Brooke instituted a system of traveling district officers whose duty it was to keep track of conditions in the remote areas of Iban country where residents in recent years had been too busy to tour. This was an attempt to restore the old style of rule by personal contact. At the same time the government persuaded Iban chiefs in the Rajang area to agree on a common interpretation of customary law. Eventually the Ibans of the Second Division also accepted common *adat* codes.

When Rajah Charles Vyner Brooke relinquished Sarawak to the British crown after World War II, Iban problems had not been solved. Iban grievances against a remote central government were simply transferred to the new authority. Governors of the crown colony now addressed themselves to the whole sector of modern progressive government characteristic in the postwar world of the developing state.

A primary school class at Melugu. The teacher is an Iban who graduated in Kuching

Despite some political difficulties in accepting the new regime, especially from Malays who wished to see a restoration of the Brooke raj, the government set about extending education and communications. Establishing schools and building roads were high priorities in the period of the late 1940's and in the 1950's.

The opening of the country by modern roads and opportunities for formal education for the Ibans were two areas neglected by the white rajahs. Implicit in the ruling idea of the Brookes had been the idea of keeping the Dayaks uncontaminated by European civilization for fear of commercial exploitation by the Westerners. Oddly enough, no such qualms had been felt in relation to the very real exploitation of Ibans by the ubiquitous Chinese immigrants whom the white rajahs

encouraged in their commercial activities.

The sphere of education, then, had been one which the Brookes left to private energies, except for the promotion of a few Malay schools. As a result, little formal schooling was available to the Dayaks upriver and schools were almost completely confined to the urban areas of Kuching and Sibu. The Church of England mission and the Roman Catholics established schools attended primarily by Chinese and Malays. And the Chinese communities provided schools under a post-revolutionary system of Chinese education which was largely financed by Chinese traders. Some of these in time were Communist influenced. But Rajah Charles Brooke had not allowed Christian missions among the Moslems and had discouraged any such attention to the Ibans.

Singing class at Melugu primary school

Calisthenics play a prominent part in the school curriculum

The feast of departed spirits in a longhouse where Western dress has replaced indigenous costume

"I am at a loss to know," he wrote in 1966, "how a mission could be really successful in its endeavours [among the Ibans]." It was only under colonial rule in 1947 that country schools began to be opened and Ibans as well as other Dayaks were encouraged to enrol their children.

Ibans, as we have noted, have seldom pushed their children in education, tending always to take a permissive view and following the wishes and whims of the children themselves. Yet it is in education that the urbanized Iban is distinguishable from his more primitive brother of the interior. A very real barrier between the two begins to be obvious not only in education but in the whole habit of living and thinking that is changing the life of the downriver Ibans.

Yet attachment to the longhouse among the urban and 'expatriate' Ibans is still very much alive. Iban youths return proudly in Western dress to their home village to display their wealth, status, and sophistication and to revel for a short time in their new prestige. But they soon sense a gap between their new habits and traditional practices, for they have learned to question many of the tribal ideas and tend to treat them with disdain. For this reason there exists more than the usual generation gap between urbanized sons and daughters and their longhouse parents, a cleavage which is undoubtedly mutually painful.

This barrier between the returned Iban youths and their village relatives ought not to be exaggerated. Many an Iban youth returning to the home *bilek* can hardly wait to take off Western cloths and get back

Traditional sword with hornbill feathers, and Western clothes—the longhouse headman attends a feast

into simpler and more comfortable dress. For some of these it is not too difficult to divest themselves of other Western habits as well. Some Sarawak Rangers home on leave from military service in the jungles of northern Malaya are, in a sense, the modern counterparts of the nineteenth-century warriors returning from pirate expeditions.

The citified Iban, usually educated at least to the secondary level, has a very modern outlook indeed. Less so the Ibans who inhabit some of the downriver longhouses, a little too close to the disrupting influence of the towns. These longhouses are not yet converted to modern ways, nor have their tenants divested themselves of traditional tribal systems. The result is frequently a depressing combination of plastic and tin-can modern and the decaying old. These dirty, unkempt

villages, ramshackle constructions of bamboo garnished with galvanized iron and linoleum, have indeed the conveniences of electricity, bottled soft drinks, glass windows, and perhaps a pump and piped-in water. But on a visit to such surroundings one longs either for the completely modern town house or for the remote upriver longhouse with its hanging skulls and smoking oil lamps, whose split bamboo floors and ironwood roof have scarcely heard the sound of the pocket transistor.

In spite of the frequent and incongruous mixture of modern and old, the cultural impact of the outside world upon traditional Iban ways has been quite gradual. No cultural shock waves have hit the majority of Iban longhouses, and nowhere is the modernizing influence upon

Building a road through the jungle

Individual prefabricated houses at Melugu replace the old longhouses

A modern family home of termite-resistant timber under construction

Men walking to their work on the rubber plantations in the early morning

Public spigots take the place of the river as the source of water in new developments

On the steps of a new family home

Timber extraction on a large scale is new to Sarawak

Log ratts ready for the journey down the Lupar River to the sea

The health services promote baby shows, with prizes for the healthiest infants

Government officials explaining to longhouse people how to vote in a forthcoming election

Unloading durians to be transported to Kuching for sale

Longhouse dwellers in Western dress under the skull trophies of former headhunting days

tribal custom as intense as appears to be the case in some African communities. The process of modernization is similar to that in Africa, but in numbers and size the world of the upper Rajang River is not comparable to the South African veld, and Sibu is not by any means Johannesburg, nor is Kuching like Capetown. By great good fortune, too, intense feelings of race do not complicate the picture in the process of modernization among the Ibans of Sarawak. It is an upheaving phenomenon, but the shock waves are really ripples. Nowadays one sees nearly as many Ibans in town—in Kuching and Sibu and Simanggang—as must be left upriver in the longhouses. Most are young, and many permanently reside and work in town. The rest visit town frequently to shop and see relatives and friends. They cannot be distinguished by their dress, for Western shirt and trousers are standard for Dayak, Malay, and Chinese. Only the visiting women stand out, tending still to wear the native sarong and cotton jacket even in town.

While resistance to change among the upriver Iban communities is marked, it is not altogether true to say, as some people have, that Ibans are unwilling to try other ways of life. Nor has the tradition of hill rice cultivation prevented fairly large numbers from taking up swamp rice growing as an occupation. Some of the ritual forms and farming methods of the hill paddy have been retained, however. But most important, swamp rice farming represents a settled way of life, and its potential yield at harvest is much greater than that of hill paddy. Ibans in numbers are now moving into the extractive industries of the oil fields and mines as permanent workers, not just as itinerants. More and more secondary school graduates are finding their way into government and business offices, and in the 1960's the first crop of Iban university students returned from study in Australia, England and North America to take up government posts and teaching jobs. The 1970 census will undoubtedly reveal that the 1960's was a decade of very real change and upheaval.

For the Ibans, a basic part of the change is that modernization has brought them into competition for employment with the Malay and Chinese and made a place for them in the urban scene. So long as the Ibans were rural longhouse dwellers they offered no real challenge to Chinese and Malays in the world of business and government. But moving into town and seeking employment, the young educated Ibans must now pit their skill against the usually more experienced Chinese. For the Ibans as a people it may well be a losing battle, since Chinese are growing in numbers faster than they are, and mainly at their expense. A demographic study of 1966 predicted that by 1985 Ibans will comprise not one-third but only one-quarter of the population of Sarawak. And the Chinese will have increased from 31 to 40 percent of the total.

That the Ibans as a tribe apart from other Dayaks will eventually lose their identity is the almost inescapable conclusion. The processes of urbanization and diversification in occupation—the discarding of the old tribal way of life—are slowly but surely proceeding. The pressures of Chinese population increase and competition will very likely force the Ibans into the melting pot with other Dayak peoples, and only in the most remote upriver areas will an Iban society remain. The tribal way of life among the Ibans of Sarawak is indeed a vanishing world.

This book is a joint production of John Weatherhill, Inc., of New York and Tokyo, and Serasia Ltd., of Hong Kong. Layout and typography by Bert Gallardo. Type composed by Asco Trade Typesetting Ltd., Hong Kong. Plates engraved and printed in offset by Nissha, Kyoto. Bound at the Makoto Binderies, Tokyo. The typeface used is Monophoto Univers.

DS646
.32
f.I2W73

2486

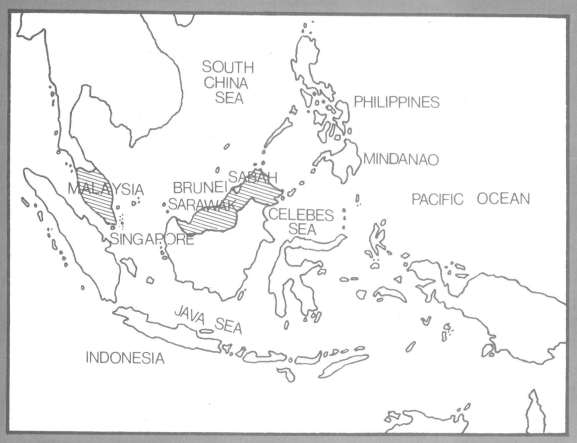

SOUTH CHIN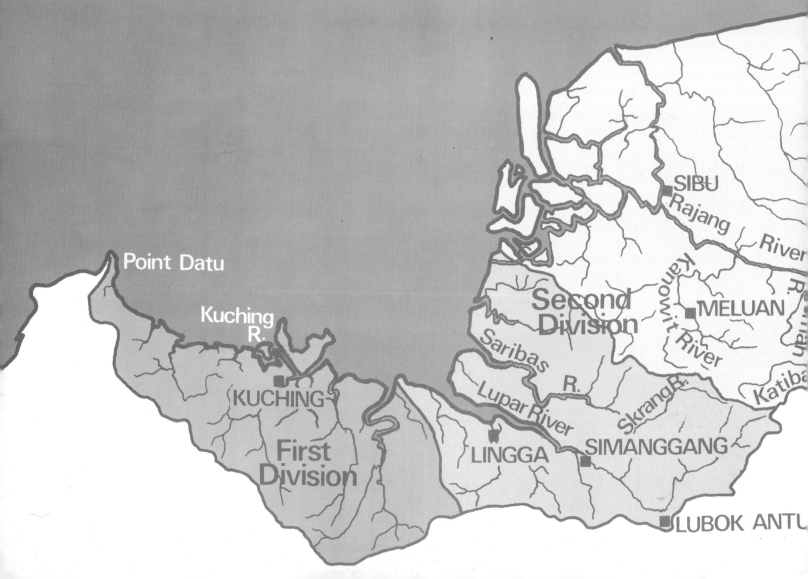